The
(3oo Poems)

Written By: J. Arthur Ferguson

Inspired by: Songwriters of the Past
This is a...
FERGUSONPOETRYPROJECT

(Credits towards the Co-Authors)
Prelude

It never ceases to amaze me... the amount of time I spend thinking about nonsense throughout the week. The wasted hours. Amidst the studies and the workloads, the chores and the bills, the relationships and partnerships, I can hardly find time to do what I love, which is to write songs that tell stories of what we have seen. There is a desire to share the love, to share the music, and to share how these things coincide. I have had the opportunity to do some wonderful things in my short time, but what is time anyways? A musician is a master of time!

Since the year 2000, or year ZERO (0), we have written over a thousand songs, we have told thousands of stories, sang thousands of songs, and we have learned time and time again that we will never scratch the surface of all that is true knowledge. All I know is that the time spent with the ones I love is precious and minimal. I think back to all who taught me Love and the Language of Music.

From the hood-rats in Carriage Park, to the geniuses of John's Creek, the friendliness of Cumming and my friends of Forsyth, my African and European amigos in Evan's Farms and the point where lives cross. Los Amigos and the Sagas of Man. To the men of Franklin that led me on the Brother's Road, to the dogs of Duluth and the Common Senseless, to the sin in Athens and Bearcat, and the Fun in Fayetteville with DIAB, to the peace in Peachtree City and forever Cougar Love! Also, to the boys of Battery Lane in Nashville, TN! My heart is with all those Giant's whose shoulders I have had the honor to stand on.

We use our actions, we use our voice, and we allow ourselves to be labeled. We do not condemn; only love. I have had the honor to speak with authority. I have had the honor to take wonderful stages in the strangest of places. I am ready to continue towards the dream. I am excited to continue towards the Great Pearl, the Pearl of great value, and the Pearly Gates themselves. We do this through love and music, food and poetry, alongside fellowship and faith.

The only condition is that when you fall in love... you will not be able to fall half-heartedly. Keep in mind that music is simply the language of Love. Keep in mind that together we have access to something that is beyond mortal man. I am not one who believe in magic, but if I were to identify the most magical thing about my time on earth it is the love that has been instilled in me by all of those who have spent time with me. I wish I had better means to communicate my appreciation, but I feel music is the only way.

Music is the only thing in my life that I see as truth. Music is the only thing that truly connects me to what we have called our creator. Music is the only thing that has given me true insight towards spirituality and mystic understanding. I am stubborn, but not with music. Worship alone lies me in the hands of God. The smile on my lover's face when I sing her my song... does it even compare to that of the maker when I sing for him? Her smile is something I would kill for, so what of my maker?

I digress into the world of Poetry, the world of song, and the world of Love. Many poets have come and gone and I am beyond grateful to join the line behind the men and women who have inspired me to become who I am today. I hope this message finds you delight. This book is dedicated to those who are in search of spiritual growth through music. This philosophy that balances physical, mental, and social health is called, "The Heart of David"!

Thanks to the dozens of Co-Authors: (specifically) Bryan Lee Mays, Benjamin David Boyd, and Kolton Ray Stooksbury for making me who I am today. Continue pursuing healthiness and happiness with the Heart of David in the forefront of thought. Let the Lord of Love and Light forever be your guide.

TABLE OF CONTENTS

MESSAGE FOUR

PART THREE (B)-JOSHUA AND THE SPIRIT OF MOSES

PART ONE...
The Course of Abraham

Welcome

Let us take this time to remember all who came before us. Let us take this time to remember how we all got here. Since the dawn of man, we have been pushing and pushing to get to where we are today. This collection of writings is to reveal how we are going to spend our time. This collection of writings is meant to reveal how we can in our turn build upon the mighty Foundation. We stand in the bible belt. We stand here on Southern Ground.

There was a time before the foundation. Thousands of years of history within an eternity of pursuance and growth. There was a time before us. There will be time after us. But, while we are here let us recognize this rock we stand on, and let us build upon it. The structure and the vision that will be supported by the Foundation is known as the Heart of David.

Musician's Prayer

God, please bless my music that it might glorify your name
May using it to serve you always be my AIM
Let it be a witness to your majesty
And love
And remind us that you're watching from your throne above
May others see your beauty in every note they hear,
And when they hear my music may they feel your presence near
Oh Lord, I ask for guidance in everything I do
And I pray you will make my music an instrument for you!

Technological Efficiencies

It is the duty for a leader of worship to create an atmosphere of prosperity
The rallentando of worship is now over
May we raise the praise alongside the rate and pace of
Technological efficiencies!

I was in an empty space. Completely nothing. And so I became, as one would imagine. I noticed I could see. I looked in amazement as enigma revealed herself to me. I moved along. I was in space. Appearing one after the other, lights began to shine. Millions of them were dancing in the sky. Each had its own unique movement as if each individual was trying to tell me something. It was as if this light wanted to acquaint itself with me. Color. A ball of color, which was white. Beside it lay red, yellow, and blue. They were being reflected in multitude by the mirror sitting behind the holes of everything. Amber waves crashed as my back was to the oceanic abyss that was everything. The holes began to build pressure allowing them to grow significantly. I became the color; I became the dance; I became a man. As I entered into the world my eyes were damaged by the light, so now I crawl with shattered vision until I learn to walk. I pray to see again.

She looked down on the twenty-fourth day of the eleventh month in confusion because it was Her birthday. That night she sang a song.

1. Something More

Feel safe as I watch you sleep
Get warm as our two skins meet
As you drift my mind will stay and pray for you

OH! How you remind me that there are better days!
Especially when this life seems to be less than fake
To know that I can count on you when all is said and done!
It allows my every day that goes
To subtly know
It belongs to something more than this!

I will be brave for liberty and for states
I will come home to surf upon my lover's waves
So maybe we will talk and not fight... just for tonight
Because every day that goes
I subtly know
We indeed belong to something more than this!

Lord, if you can please show me your one true way
To that place where you rest beyond the grave
Because my soul will not stop until it finds you
Even though I am deeply scared of the truth
And so, even as my last days continue to go
I continuously know
We do belong to something more than this!

Pick me! Pick me up! Put me down! I want to figure how to carry myself around. I need to remember what I have seen. There was that moment being born into everything. I try to enjoy the moment while it lasts. I know this life is short, and passed me is more past. Time becomes a very real thing as she obsesses over her victory over the living dead. I heard a whisper, "This is only the beginning. Be Patient. Be Brave. Be Strong. Use your head, and listen to your heart. Do not be afraid of what tomorrow will bring; seize the day. Today is a day we should celebrate." Though I believe we should celebrate every day. Today is the day! Today is my birthday!

2. <u>Be Not!</u>

Who are you?
What would you allow my love?
Would you allow some demon to crawl into your heart?
>This cannot be right for you
>No one this young made it out this far
>Besides you!

You may free your lips for you are no longer wounded for me
I have healed you, and brought you safely home
>Because I knew this was not right for you
>Only I should take you out this far

Be not one who would be sold or lost within his or her thoughts!
Be not one who puts themselves in situations not meant for us!

Healthiness is happiness. By holding on to hate, by holding on to the regret and the shame, love cannot break through. As a seedling waiting to surface after germination, I am waiting for this love to break through. The soil of my soul has been cleansed and saturated with the proper minerals. Now, it is time to watch the fields peak with baby green for the sun has come. The sun has revealed itself to us in majesty by providing healthy light to complement our sacred love.

There is one race, and it is the human race. Amongst the field of many weeds we have a tree that bears great fruit. The tree is man and the field is earth. The fruit are our sons and the weeds are our enemies. Although we are surrounded we will prevail because we are in favor. Our enemies include war, religion, hate, and time.

3. Empathy

Life is based on the perception in which you see it
One day your tower may have a niveous reflection
It may be strangely tall
The next day it may be blown away
Blackening the world in its ash and smog
It is up to you to see past this
Look for a smile!
They will help you keep your head up along the way
        I know if you could feel this love
        You would understand everything that is above
        If you were to search everywhere with your lamp lit
        And heart proud
        You could turn out to be light within the darkness
        All around
For you would not fear the boss if you would get to know him
Do you believe that it is right for the heart to go astray?
You say you care, but do you truly show it?
Do you want your short life in eternity to mean nothing?
        I know that if you felt it
        I could show you what my heart is all about
        I would open up and never quit
        May purity lift your dirty feet far off the dirty ground!
Sometimes life's pain can be far too real
But you cannot just let your heart wander
For you will have to catch it one day
For if your heart's ember is but a dwarf gleed in the distance
It will be very hard to catch
You may be too old and too tired
You may be too weak and not very fast

Sing with me. "JAM!" Oh, nothing makes me feel more alive than music. I love swaying to the beat, and I love lifting up the mood as we settle into a heavenly groove. Nothing gets to me like jamming.

From above, a touch will lead you up to love. There stood the prize of prize reflecting in my eyes. My whore, my feet will walk up to your nest as you plead your life to this. I long to see that face again. "Do not worry about me..." she says. It escalades into a different place, towards better days.

4. I Long to See Your Face

My heavy burdened hands will rise
To pour your blood upon the sand
And no one will be able to see through your bruised eyes
Not even you!
These dark dreams have come in the night
       I will bear arms my friend
       And I will create wounds upon your hands
       Through me, everyone will see what you hide
       And in your mind is where you will die!
Every whore, every knee, will bow within your nest
I will plea my life for this as long as I can see your face
From above, a touch will lead you up to my love
You gave your life for this so all can see your face
       For an entire human race
       Everyone will see your face

My hands are tied my dearest friend. I must continue to search for the Heart of David. I am young and naïve. It could have been said that, "This boy will never make it into adulthood." I am reckless, careless, and selfish, yet it was unknown to me. I was living day by day in my own head.

It is because of the love instilled in me that I was lucky enough to survive. It was because of the strengths given to me by my brothers that I had the wits to get through the shadows. It was not until the first message sent by Joshua did I feel the true presence of the Lord, and the hope he promises is real.

5. My Friend

I know you know this but I am thinking of you within my room
As my mind races and dances within this fiery place
I feel your eyes on me
Though they are seeing right through me
I recall your voice whispering, "Go!"
　　　　And so I go
I will find my place within this world

I was warned to not let a pretty girl get inside of my head
Move me up! Move me down! Love me! Love me!
I know she sees me rolling around in her bed
It took only a second for her feet to leave the ground
　　　　　　But do not worry about me my friend
　　　　　　You will see my face again
　　　　　　We are not alone, and I will not let go
　　　　　　My love for you will never end

What is unconditional love? As I began to date and date, and of all of the pretty girls I would meet, I could not seem to ever find happiness in myself. Once my peers were all of age they began to mingle and experiment. And so I mingled… and she mingled…

Overflowing
Overflowing is this cup of love
I pity any man who does not drink him some
Bound is my heart with this love
And sad is my spirit for those who refuse to come
Now happiness, for a brief moment, is allowed within my head
I will entertain the spirit that allows this
It makes me feel more human than usual
I wish this feeling would remain forever
This love that is here is welcomed to stay whenever
For as long as it desires!

And so she flees to the west…

Obsession. A decade of dedication towards a person I am told I do not deserve. Hatred has been thrown my way multiple times now. I have been told I will never be good enough, but my Lord disagrees. We all long to have love, and to hold love, but I will never have or hold the people I still love but who were taken from me.

When I turned 17 I was introduced to infinity. I was taught love and I was shown a glimpse of truth. It came in the form of unconditional love. I am still imperfect. I will always make mistakes, and I will be shocked if not at least one sin is committed today.

I will always love him, her, them and most importantly you!

6. <u>Inchworm</u>

Travel long; travel hard; get caught in the wind
Do not be afraid of judgment day for it will not be the end
But will you find yourself tied to the ground
      Reaching up to the sky with floating all around?
And as you find your purpose... will you save it?

From each step a scent is left
It takes you back to a place that once took your breath
But we are all given a choice to carry on
To leave the past in the past, your future's what is strong
      And inch-by-inch you will struggle
      To find what is beautiful

Then go and find a place deep in the woods to settle down
You can break away from the world
It is perfect, safe and sound
But you alone cannot make it out
Out of this world that has kept your heart abound
And as you take your last breath you will see what is beautiful

And now he is gone; there is no way he is turning back
      Into a bird or butterfly to fight against the wind
To be alone there is a timely cost
Your life will be gone and attached will be a feeling of great loss
      But now the earth does not bind you
Eternity is beautiful!

These times recorded at the Warehouse with a dear friend. I believe him to be a mutual friend of almost everybody. We talk of three percent. We play the rest. This is the way life should be. We should all be able to enter into that state of mind where the world is your empire. But OH do we grow tired. Day by day it takes its toll, and I tell my love that loving someone like me is not the way to go, but you never know.

I have very mixed views about what to do next. There is a slight hesitation on my part, and for this I am sorry. I refuse to pause. I must keep moving forward and if I wander off path it is because I felt in jeopardy. The course is dangerous. This was known. But I move forward without thinking about anything although I am thinking about everything.

7. Rich Man

A lady with a purple face
She sits atop her castle to this day
She is waiting for a change
She wants to be released from her life that is worthy of complaint
May every angel fight for her tonight!
May they save every soul that cannot provide...
> Every soul out of my sight
> No Devil is welcomed inside
> NOT TONIGHT!
Millions of cries upon my mind
Not one cares for a simple good-bye
Worse than a warrior who has lost his mind
To: measly Pagan gods
> He gives a sacrifice
> A rich man who knows not what is right
> Remunerates via the innocent blood upon his hide
> A rich man will drown tonight
Within himself, his sins, his pride

And so the rich man will ask me how I find such happiness in such shaky circumstance, and it is because I am not bound by possession. What would it take for me to lose myself in the things I own? What would it look like?

8. Incunabula

He travels through his life
People see him on autopilot thinking, "He is not free."
        And life does not wait
She is full of life so there must be
An explanation for the shame we see upon her face

He pulls and tugs upon his hair
Into the mirror he looks and he stares
She wakes up to a man to find
No more love is living in his eyes
        She cries and she sleeps

And there comes a sign for them to find
And it is within the OPEN
Neither one of them will yet see
But he is right and she is right
If you can wait, then they will be

Each day their love will grow at a rapid pace
Love will be lurking all among their faces
        Now time must do its thing
They need courage within these next few steps
He must save her from the man she is with
        And OH! When their eyes meet...
        Incunabula!

They will be thrown chest into chest and will know no reason
The stage has been set for them to find peace
They have been given signs
We all are given these signs!

        I knew it! I knew it! I am not the one. I cannot be the one. I knew
this from the beginning, but I was far too stubborn to admit it. I constantly
pray for forgiveness even to this day. I am just an ordinary man. In my
defense, I hold a love that is far too heavy to hold on my own. And so, I let
her go. I let her fall into the arms of another. I say goodbye within my heart
as it opens again for the first time in a long time. I am finally open to find
new love.

9. Sweet Soul

She thinks,
I will carry you away as a beauty shot into the heart
But I wonder if you will stay or will you travel long and far?
I know a drunken man will pose and follow me up to my steps
But I will not bring him home
I will not clean his drunken mess!

He speaks
"I know I seem to be weary
But you are so lovely and I need you right now!
For your unique beauty has overwhelmed
And has brought this drunken man down!"

She will call him a spineless man and a drunken man
She will say that she would never carry him home
She will say, "You will just leave me and never call me"
She will say, "What are you? But a drunken man!"

He prays, "Lord, help me! Lord, Help me!"

"Oh Sweet!" he will say, "Oh sweeeet, sweet soul!
Please carry me home.
I will never leave thee. I will always call thee.
In my heart, your love is doing something to me."

And so she carried him home as a beauty shot within the heart
She needed someone to stay
She needed to mother every wound and every scar
Though the drunken man did pose following her up to the steps
She kindly took him in and cleaned him
That foolish drunken man's mess!

I have witnessed some foolish things. Where is this life thing going? What is the point of this foolish world? Love? What is love? I feel it. I love it, and I hate it. It makes me happy, and it also makes me terribly sad. I feel like I can lift the world with a finger, and then the next day I could not even pick myself up. This life swings hard to the left and then hard to the right. It repeats and repeats. This chaos can drive a man insane without something to assist in the weight. Not even the Savior of Christianity could carry his own cross all the way to Calvary.

10. Once

Even the wisest man cannot truly see through your eyes
Every sinful life attempts to push the wrong as the right
Once I had pleaded, "Lord, please take my life!"
Would it be noticed if I hung myself as a sign?

Laughs were turning into cries
Some cries back into laughs and that was alright
Once I lay within a field counting diamonds in the sky
Thoughts of you knowing every name was enough to get me high

But Lord, do you see how she moves?
Lord, is this truly what I am to call mine?
I hope and I pray because I do not trust my own eyes
I hope and I pray, "Lord, keep me in line for her!"

There was a time when I worried about getting old
But now, I do not believe that matters anymore
Just once, I will be in my prime
All of my time... all of my life... once... in my prime

          I read these words five years later, and it makes my
heart happy to know questions are answered. Do not put your future into
the hands of situation! Put your faith in God and in God alone. I am now
truly in my prime, and I am full of energy though I am tired all of the time.
My father tells me that is life. Soon, I will lose the energy, and I will grow
more tired. This will be okay because I will be more full of love than I am
today! Oh how this love grows!

A Good-man Prayer

I will wait...
I will wait until you are ready
I will climb...
To get where you need me to be
I will walk...
I will walk upon this ocean
I will die...
Only to come back to life for love
I will be...
A whirlwind of fire on you
I will be...
A flashflood to carry you away
I will look...
To see what is coming
I will preach...
So I can keep you up
I will not fear...
Though this river is growing higher
And even though this path is very narrow
I will not fear.
Because our Lord is always enough
God, I see it. Allah, I feel it.

I write Allah as if I know what that is. I write God as if I know what that is... I began asking the one question that has taken me where I am today! I began asking the one question that will take me where I need to go! I began asking questions! This one question is the most important question in the world to me because it will take me to all corners of the earth either physically or metaphorically. Is Jesus God?

It does not matter if you have an answer or not. It does not matter who is right or who is wrong. It is not a competition by any means. I ask this question because I have to. This is my purpose. This one question is the reason I live, and this one question is the reason I write. Every day I feel like my answer changes, yet every day I know I grow closer to the end of my days, and this makes me happy because I know one day I will find out the truth. This love is real and it is irresistible.

I continue to play the guitar, I begin to play the saxophone, I learned to play the piano, I dabble on the mandolin, I roll upon the banjo, I laugh and play the harp, I slap upon the bass, and I sing soft into the condenser... for now.

11. Wasted Colors

I am searching for you
Are you searching for me?
I am tripping over wasted colors that even blind men can see
Evanescing is a family spawning no man able to herd sheep
It is as light that fades into darkness
It is like watching darkness lead

I also see few rich men feeding the hungry
Could I be filled with such greed?
To never give one simple answer
To always be planting barren seeds
      As if it is for show?

And so it is hard to find a reason
When so many live their lives without any change
They are tying themselves down!
They want everything to remain the same

But it is not hard at all to find a reason
When life is truly lived you always change
And NOTHING can tie you down
Nothing will ever be the same

I know that I can change something
I can give all of my love unto a stranger
All for free
Not even for you or for me
But for free
Even though this love is for you and for me

Freedom! Freedom! Freedom! I have freedom, and it can never be
taken away. I can serve for free. I can love for free. My mind can wish, and
dream, and love and it is all for free. Cursed are those who strip free-will.
Cursed are those who believe they are not free no matter the circumstance.
Cursed are those who are bound by possession. Cursed are those who
neglect their duties and the will of God to pursue stoic hedonism as if the
world owes you something. Cursed are those who lie, cheat, and steal.
Cursed are those who play politics while the rest work their fingers to the
bone to earn a fair day's wage. Cursed are those who continue to conspire
against those who fight to be genuine/ those who fight for honesty within
the art. Cursed are those who deny Love.

12. <u>You Are Enough</u>

I spawned as mirth within your dreams
And now we are growing very close
Just as faint comes into focus
Or as a mortal man becomes a ghost
I will forever be waiting for you my love
I want you and only you. That is enough.
You are enough.

Oh, how I wish that you could see me my little girl
I watch you every time that you wish by your mama's well
If genies of lamps and wishes were real
Imagine how good it would feel?
To wish for your world
Not for the diamonds, the silvers or the pearls
But to see me, and I see you, my girl
Every day you could awake without a care in the world
And where would you go from there?
Well, how do you feel words describe one's deepest fears?
Chasing beauty and bones will only lead you alone
So I will attempt to share with you all that is in my head
Your mother is my best friend
You will see we are one
As you cast a reflection in the mirror
And I...
I am every soft wind
I am every dream afar; I am everything that is near
One day you will go with him and disappear
The world will come to a stop and you will understand fear
He will be your home, so even when you are alone
You will have him running in circles within your head
And you will not erase me
Learn to love
All of these writings that once caused you fear
Understand one day that you will see me
You will meet me...
Maybe somewhere far... Maybe somewhere near

Love...love... it has been here long enough
He will want you. As you both grow old... as I do
It will start in your dreams so close.
From faint into focus until he proposes
Just know I am always here with you my love
I will always love you. And that is enough. You are enough.

If I have you, girl, I will never need too much.
If I have you, every day, I will say you're enough
Because You are enough.

13. ALPHA

May the Eye show me everything that it can see!
I want to see beyond the lies surrounding my entirety
Vinous eyes of love are calling out my name
They say, "I need you here. I will cry if you cannot stay!"
   But if I love all people as I should
   I should never second-guess all that is good
   I will never say, "I wish I could, or I should have…"
   I will say, "A foolish man would say he can't!"
For everyone knows the Eye is good

I remember every night I have spent
I am waiting for a call to open up my mind once again
Could I fall in love?
Tonight?
   With her vinous eyes of love
   She stirs the fire within my soul
   An ember dripping amber like honey
   Made by the maker
She is the only one to take me in with all my ways
I know this is due to the Alpha!
I know this is due to the Omega!

So many life changes… Every year seems as if it is a whole new life. Every year I feel as if I enter a new dimension. Few things remain. I am not even the same anymore. I have changed significantly. Friends always come and go. Women come and go. I could never have assumed that I would be where I am today. New things are coming to me all of the time. I do not necessarily care for these shiny new things. These things do not mean anything when compared to those who I love. Material possession is a modern curse on man. "Carry your things at all times". The phone, the keys, the wallet, the plastic, and all of the other non-living things that rule my life are driving me insane.

I think of being a child with no phone and no problems. I admire the feats we achieved by socially connecting, mentally connecting, and physically connecting all of humankind. We have an ability today that has never been known in history ever. We are Generation One. We are the turn of the tide. We are the revolution. We are the beginning of true globalization, and we will not stop there as long as the Universe allows us to exist.

14. <u>Anymore</u>

Is it hard for you?
Can you trust in a frenetic love?
A love that promises to never say bye
Or a love that constantly compromises?
To me, there is no answer
I will let time be the judge
To me I ask, "Why do you care?
Why must you insist?"

Close ones will say, "He fought and he lost."
But any more talk would not get any point across
There exists an illusion that time holds all of the answers
So time will be my friend, and I will keep it close
        I will not disagree when wise men speak
        It is known they have seen a better way
        "By magic he plays his music," they say
        He plays the music playing in my head

I will be dead and gone
Before that magic guides me through those doors
And my heart will not be sore anymore
Anymore

     Poof. There was nothing, and now there is something. It is hard for me to believe in magic. I am a fan of witchcraft and wizardry, but I do not believe in it. I do believe in miracles beyond my control. I do not believe man can willingly access magic to do his own bidding. Selflessness is about the only "magic" I need to be a believer of the light. So then, what is this light that takes me away towards Dreamland?
     Life is a dream. If it is not a dream that you may not be living right. This is not your fault. We have failed you. The children of God have failed you. You did not fail yourself. If your life is anything less than a wonderful dream I am sorry. If your life is anything less than a dream the people of God failed. You may be living in sin, and you may be living in an unfair situation filled with hate and abuse, but it is not your fault. It is not God's fault. It is the corrupt men who allowed the pursuit of money to cross the lines of human morality. It is the fault of men and women who chose themselves over their family, and for this I am sorry.

15. <u>Dreamland</u>

Welcome aboard!
   You are on the Dreamland
Please consanguine with all of your high friends
   I feel so light from all of this drinking
How I wish to keep on with this high thing

You ask me to go where I have never been
You ask me to speak out against any shadow
You tell me I will not be seen unless the sun can see me
You tell me I will not be able to speak unless I sing
You say it is not okay to confuse your night with the day
   You show me how dangerous it is to live that way
You have shown me how many lose their lives within every day
You have shown me the loss of time
That will catch up to us all the same

I have seen the traveling waters that flow underground
They have become sound, and now they turn into colors
I can see every friend I have ever encountered
   After all is said and done, I will return
   Under the sun is where I have made a home
   It is where I must go now!

Holiday Seasons
Viridescent nature foreshadows the coming of spring
During the spring, rubricate the house to foreshadow your healthy garden
Yield fresh berries and fruits: Strawberries and Apples
Jar and Preserve them for your fellow neighbors for the fall
Use these colors and this kinship to prepare for winter
The Holiday seasons will flourish with friends and family
Clothed in Organic Red and in Pure Green

16. Flow Together and Say Goodbye

Hello my dearest friend
Try to not lose yourself today
I cogitate that it is indeed within the darkness
You wonder how truly far it could be
        I know you want to explore, to see what is out there
        It is a damn shame most people do not care
        I believe I could have saved you...
        Damn it! Please do not die on me
Can you see how I believe in every little thing?
Is it wrong that I dream?
I am. We will.
This is the night to come alive
We will rise up with the sun
And become one
        One for all, all for one, my lover has lost her mind
        She says that she will see me on her way down
        She says plenty of people do the same
        I do not believe they truly know their chances
        Not all will have a safe fall into my arms
        Though I could have saved you
        Please do not die on me!
Would you let me crawl into your soul?
Within every nerve could I take my control?
I could crumble every wall, and you would never feel this pain
Once I reach my destination your legs will cause you to drop
This will happen when I go down on you
        I feel we are so in tune
        You will shake me up until I just break through
        We go around and around
        Until our flesh is one and once you are done
        You will dig your nails down deep
        Sweat will be dripping as after a run
And so you will see why I believe in every little thing
We will flow into one from two
You and I, me and you
I will go down

I will say good-bye to all
I will see you when it rains
I will chase after the dark
I will lose my one escape
        When I am gone some will say preachers are to blame
        Do not let them take away your Heaven!
        Do not let them mix their fire with your rain!
        OH! When she is gone...
To put all of the chips in one basket
To throw all of your soldiers on one boat!

To sacrifice others at the expense of personal victory.
To change the world by stepping on the shoulders of the weak!
>> He gave it all. I gave it all.
>> We lost her. We gave her up.
>> We might as well have sold her to the highest bidder
>> We let her be used by the masses
This was not love. This mentality quickly shifts into shame.
Do not listen to these lies. Do not let the enemy win.
>> We go around and around in infinity.
>> And so I question everything.

Not only is this a combination of two poems written as a teenager, but it was foreshadowing of pain I knew I would experience being in a relationship that I knew I did not belong in. There have been many songs written within withering relations. There have been many songs written about the aftermath of those relations that did not succeed. Though a decade has past I begin searching for love in the strangest corners of the earth. I am slowly beginning to realize my purpose, and if the Lord rewards me with one more opportunity to love someone whole heartedly, I would proudly accept.

I must realize that my heart does not belong to one single individual. It can never belong to just one because I chase after the Lord God with all my soul, all my heart, and all my mind. I attempt to humble myself on a daily basis as I pursue the Heart of David in the form of a song and dance man. I love being able to play music in front of people. I love the fact I can make people happy by playing music. I am blessed to be able to impress musicians with my talents, and I am blessed I can direct that focus back on to the Lord for giving the ability to do the things I do.

Yes, I am the one who has put in over ten thousand hours of playing music and writing songs. And yes, I am the one who has dug down deep for the will to go on when things got tough. But I remember! I remember that the Lord is the one who gave me Passion to write and record. I remember that the Lord gave me strength and patience to work towards tomorrow. I know I have had the experience that makes me the best candidate to do what I am doing, but I am still in search for the unconditional love. I hold this love in one facet or another. I know I should love all of my brothers and sisters as the Lord loves us, but will this love be returned? Will this love be received by the material world? Would this love be received? Could this love be received?

17. Here It Goes

You should be the only one. For all of my time
Let me take your hand so you may open my eyes
I feel that you are everything that is wise
You are so far beyond the larrikin wearing a disguise
    I wish I could know what you are thinking
    I wish I could know how close is too close
    I wish I could ask all of your friends
        But would they truly know?
Please wait! Just look at me!
What if I brought you one of every flower?
    and said, "How about now?"
    Would you then be proud?
I know these earthly signs should never be taken for granted
For whenever the moon wakes up we all beautifully know
And so here I will go, as every soul will go on its own
They must forget all they were told, and all they have learned
    For this love to work
And they will cease mysophobic behavior once you are close
    This will occur during the last days of our earth!

    I spent two years in the music capital of the world. I began to read the Bible. I do not know why I decided to do this, but I read and read over the course of two years. I only completed the Old Testament during this time, but it did not stop there. I absorbed it. I fell in love with the stories. I grew attached to the characters in a way I was not expecting. I continued to fight for the desire to understand more and more about the history of humanity. From Will Durant's collection of writings all the way back to the dawn of man and Albert Einstein's, "The World as I Know it". Modern News only captures what it wants to capture just as fairy tales always have happy endings.

    Life is not always a fairy tale. A boy has a crush. A boy pursues his crush. He writes her a song, and he brings her flowers. She laughs at the boy. He wants to figure out the best path towards that. From spending time with World War Two Veterans to getting divine inspiration from religious leaders in the world's bible belt. The men of men begin to give their insight. This is just two years after Joshua revealed himself to me.

    He called out the woman to my left. He called out the woman to my right. He bestowed the Spirit of Moses upon me, and blessed me with Leadership. From prophecy, from heartbreak, from mentorship, from internship, I have acquired interdisciplinary skills unique to me. I thank God. You who are also unique should thank God because one day your reflection on the outside will not reflect the inside. When this happens you will need something to turn to. I pray you do not turn inward. I pray you turn to your brothers and sisters. I pray you turn to the grace and mercy of the Lord. I pray you Follow the Course. I pray you realize that God is Love, and Love is Real.

18. <u>Mister</u>

Extended conversation meant to lead him right
It taught him how to fight during the beforetime
Never let your guard down boy
Understand these joys to be a man
       Lay your personal future down by your side
       You may pray to God for it every night
       Lay your brother's dreams in front of you
       Allow them to be your stars
       Allow them to be your guide
Now take my hand, you may hold it tight
Forever is this love. A concept so very nice
So even if I am wrong, but I think I am right
You will love me until I die?
       Verbigerately forget those rules taught every day
       This world is for taking and for play
       Have a thalassic mind and let the ocean be your stage
       Let your many enemies become your many friends!

That heartbreak will turn into gold
Your hands will reach high towards the sky
Every mister must grow old
But his ministry must never die!
Never let their music die!

I have spent so many hours trying to master these silly tasks. I wish I could have a direct count of the amount of time that I have spent learning these random songs and memorizing these random lyrics. What is it for? To make a pretty penny...

My music is not for work. It cannot be subjected to simply making money. I truly believe music can save souls and impact those who are lost in their own minds. I will always strive to make my work better for my audience. I have sacrificed so much for my brothers and sisters. How long will it take before they see? Will I even be alive when that day comes? These are not questions I care to be answered. At least not now. For now, I desire to be with you and you alone.

19. By My Side

My lady, you have been worried all day
Vernaculate these signs and tell me
Are you alive for you? Or are you alive for me?
        She is thinking, "Why he is talking as if I should stay?"
        She wants him to stay away!
        She is sick of these games he is playing in her head
        And she is very quick
He wonders, "How does she do it?"
Can we stop?
        We are fooling around for nothing
We should talk
        I need to tell you something
Do not be scared of this. You should know I love you, you bitch

Baby!
        Talk!
If there is anything you ever need I will make it work
For you, nothing is impossible
        How she loves it
You are the one, and I am sure of it

It is okay, it is alright
I will not be alone tonight

Though I am mine
I grew up on my own, so my mind would be fine
And now,
I cannot get her out
She is breaking me down
But I love it
She is the one; I am sure of it

If it is okay, and if it is all right
Will you sleep with me tonight?
I need you by my side
I need you as my wife

What do you do when she says no? How will you handle yourself?

Reflections. Insecurities. Unparalleled confusion on the topic of young romance. How could one survive the slaughter of two immature people in a serious relationship? What would it look like for me to find someone who enjoys all of the things that I enjoy? I have such specific tastes, and every day I get more specific. Every day I get more specialized in what I do.

How could I find a woman who loves music like I do? How could I find a woman who loves cooking like I do? How could I find a woman who appreciates woodworking as I do? How could I find a woman who loves the body as I do? How could I find a woman who loves Poetry as I do? How do I find a woman that I could thoroughly study scripture with? How do I find a woman who loves building up sexual tension as I do? How could I find a woman who believes in mutual submission? How do I find a woman who will never give up when things get tough? How do I find a woman who will let me love her with everything I have? How can I find a woman who will forgive me for my mistakes with unconditional love? God will protect me and guide me. I just pray my eyes are open when that woman walks into my life.

And behold, the past will repeat itself. The past will always repeat in some fashion. It is a matter of which variables are constant. I feel that as long as I am the shifting variable then I everything else can remain the same for the sake of them. But you, my love, must change with me and we must grow together. We must become all we are meant to be for this life is so short, yet it is very much worth the living.

20. <u>On the 7th Stanza...</u>

Man's lust after gold is why God hides the gates to his Heaven
Even if the doors were wide open
These blind men would never see it
They brood in their sin and have lost all of their senses
Through poor preaching
Everything has evolved into Nothing!

Ignorance ignores every call and every sign upon the wall
But who, these days, can trust in an advertisement?
By many beds lies old leather bibles
But those ratty old things are not worth a reading
                And so God hides the gates to his Heaven

Spend your last ephemeral days chasing rainbows
On the other side
                There is only black and white where no gold resides
You may walk on ahead into darkness; blindly taking steps
Because this is your test

There will be a time to talk and a time to listen
You will be consulted on everything you have done
But will you be ready?
If I am not impressed with the way you carried yourself
                Up to your very last days, what would you say?
Would you be okay? Would you make it?
No crosses count anymore. You cannot just quit

And what if I told you that you are a big lie!
Like spinach flashing and stuck in one's teeth
Do you understand what I mean?
Those slimy hands have taken one too many things
You have been scamming the streets and just taking!

But you still have one last chance to show me what you can do
I am relying on you
There is no more breaking down
That is the fastest way into the cold ground
Unbroken you must be. All of the way to the end
                And so, I will let you go now my long lost friend...

I remember combining two old poems to form this one. I remember being angry and confused because I wanted to love so hard, but I did not know how. I wanted to discover something about myself that I wasn't ready to discover. It was not until three years later that I finally became the man that I should have been then. It was not until a year after that when I realized I am still years away from being who She needs me to be. For now, I work hard, I play hard, and I pray even harder.

Studying Andy Stanley has led me to ask very interesting questions. It takes me towards the realization that everything has a purpose, and my life specifically has purpose. I have been born with very extraordinary circumstances in a time that is hard to explain.

As I read these writings of a struggling teenager it is almost hard to relate in my present mindset. The struggles still exist, and life is absolutely harder day by day, but I when I read the writings of this lost boy I feel many mixed emotions. Some of these writings do not even seem to be written by me though the majority have been written by me alone.

Day by day this life takes its toll, and I understand that loving someone like me is not the way to go, yet the Lord will love me unconditionally. I have been shown love in far too many forms to deny it by this point. My heart, seemingly, wants to pull me astray. A new woman is beginning to enter into my life just as they have in the past. This one is different though... Unique in her own way... I can take a glimpse into her past and immediately feel anxiety. I can review her portfolio of what she wants the world to see her as, and I immediately begin to become jealous. It is strange because I do not know her. I wish to know her. We are strangely dancing around our social groups, and by this point I cannot ignore that there is something there.

I am absolutely frightened! I am still unfamiliar with many forms of love. My walls are higher than they have ever been, and I am still crushed from my last relationship. I was shown love, I have applied love, and now I am eager to succeed at it, but I am fearful that it will not happen in the stereotypical way. I will see her soon. I want to be ready. I am years from becoming the man she deserves, yet I am being given an opportunity to show her a glimpse of who I can be.

The Ways of Love

One lost soul sat beneath a tree
His heart full of love, and his mind soon to be
He thought he could conjure a way to persuade his enemies
If only they could understand his ways
Maybe if they believed "I Am" or "His name"
A heart so full of love
He opened himself up
He came for you and me
I was broken up
My head and heart filled up with love
I had not a phrase I could whisper to my friend
For it all lay within the ways

Late for work, speeding down the street
Coming down to earth can be the hardest thing
Believe me, when she cries or sings
It is heavenly to me

21. Summer Storm

Trying to wake me; wanting to take me
Being well known you cannot just let go
Golden rays have many waves
And they will cast many shadows
And knowing what I know
Will only cause puddles of red
I cannot lie down for in it I will drown
So do not try to please me
I am enjoying watching you from my balcony
I will never lock or even close my door
It is like walking out into the wind
Diving in the pool trying to find your bliss
Lord, let us sink into our lover's lips
Just like this, I will sink into my lover's lips

22. I Want to Be Alive

Let us stop
Let us stare
Let us ride now
> Let us walk
> Let us laugh
> Let us take our time now
Nobody here is waiting for the other side
The time is now; time to be wise
Drifting along this long ride
Drifting past the mourning of this life
> I want to feel alive
> Take my flesh and cut me loose
> I am the incipient of this new age culture
> For the next generations
> May you grind my bones to spark your flame!
Now, I can see that there is more to this furtive life
I had always wondered if the outside world was
> Truly halcyon and nice
There are not any people here walking around and complaining
If you can find leisure within your own pity and sadness
Enjoy your lagniappe

I must admit I am fond of the change of pace. This was the light in the darkness I was waiting for. A glimpse of a man who is not going to take no for an answer. Seeing my top five strengths of Achiever, Belief, Self-Assurance, Includer, and Learner will absolutely guide me along this path of righteousness. I hope my patience will grow alongside these strengths so I will be able to accomplish far more than these writings alone. A decade of teenage angst. A decade of unnecessary questioning. A decade of wanting to take the life of a boy who would soon become a man with a most promising future. Thank you Joshua. Your sacrifice was not in vain!

I continue my education under Eighty Years of teaching and discipleship. Although this is only a vapor compared to the teachings of Jesus, I am honored to be a part of something greater than myself. I am honored to be a part of building something greater than myself. First, a camp, and soon, a city!

23. Moiety of the Heart

I wish some things would never change
I wish I could be here for you, as our hairs turn grey
My lady, to me, you still look the same
You say do not forget to live by
      These features that make you different
They will allow you to fly
They will help you understand why I do this

Day by day life has taken its toll
Loving someone like you was absolutely the way to go
Because you have known me, you will always know me
      Ask your heart when you need to go
      That is the place to start
      That is the place that matters most
      The heart is the greatest place to start

      The Heart, as referred to in the Old Testament, is the place where all of the emotions spawn. What is in the heart will determine what comes out when things are at their best, and when things are at their worst. As my last days go, I continuously know we do belong to something more than this.

      I am listening in ways I could not before. I am seeing things in lights that I was once blind to. I am traveling to corners of this country to places I did not know existed. I am grateful for this love.

24. <u>Like You</u>

Her light shines bright in muddy waters
Her eyes give in due to a love imbued by her father
Those eyes... so brown... so cute

Lock on her dress boy and be bold!
When she undresses love will not be on hold
And the way she will move... what once was in me...
Her love... Is now in you

Do not let your light fade within smoky rooms
She will whisper something... if only you knew as I knew
She is perfect for you

My blessings are with you my dearest of friends
Her love is unique and incomparable to any other woman
Those eyes and lips that bloom... my blessings are with you
The way she will move... sempiternal... you can never lose

I wish I remembered where this came from. I cannot recall the inspiration for this writing, but I assume that it came from a place of yearning, appeasement, and acceptance. When you finally begin to let go of something that is more than a part of you. As time and space continues to expand, we are in a constant state of drifting apart less gravity takes hold of you. Gravity can pull anything together across time and space.

Maybe two people of my past will come together in a miraculous way. Maybe the last two people I would expect. Maybe I was the catalyst for an eternal love? Wouldn't that be something special!

25. Lucy

You and I could sail the world
These mellifluous words will allow you
To see everything you have wished for my girl
The propinquity of that something that is always on your mind
Will give you infinite time for your mind to frolic and find
        You must leave and never look back
        You must leave it in the past
No body is left; no body can be sold
You and me can sit and watch this sea turn gold
At midnight will be the ride for one last time
        It has been all trouble until now
        Your daddy would be proud
        At least for now
Those darkened eyes forever steal me away
From blue to brown or brown to grey, you always treat me well
And through this thin-fine air I see
You have battled and have been triumphant against Hades
        Now, no demon can contain
        Her soul will remain the same
For now, we will sit here dreaming underneath this tree
We will draw fine lines between the heavens and the seas
        Lady is my friend and she will always be
        A decorative member of my family
        She cries most every night and I cannot believe
        When she is gone out of my sight I feel I am blind
        I need my lady

What if she has already seen the world? What if I am not the one to show her these things? I must refer back to the Lord and recognize what I have been given. There is something I have that you cannot find anywhere else in the world, and it is my love. This is not to say that she could not find a powerful love in another corner of the world, or even across the street, but nonetheless it would not be my love! Only I possess my love, and only I will choose to whom that love will be placed upon.
        If only my love is what she was seeking...
If only I was her other half... I digress...

There was a point in America's history where a shot was metaphorically heard around the world. Now, literal shots are seen around the world at the speed of electricity in the palm of our hands. The people of this world now experience a new realm of freedom and of free speech. Simultaneously man has lost a perspective on privacy. Some argue it is because we are drifting apart; some claim these are early signs of man truly coming together. Neither is bad nor good, simply open to interpretation.

Facts given to us from the past declares, sides will always be chosen, war will always be around the corner, but let it be known once again that united we stand, and divided we fall. Naturally, I pray for the average American to reunite under the same stars that set us free. War is at our door. The enemy lives within our walls. The love America has to offer can disarm a soldier sent for destruction. Say Hello to your new neighbor. Love your new co-worker. Become friends with the introvert along with the extrovert. Create a superfluous love that will cause any man to become friend instead of foe. Allow variance in your everyday life. Accept man for what man is and be love! This is exciting to some men and scary to others. I am very intrigued to see how this up and coming world will sustain itself. Though the point is moot, and every answer remains an opinion, I am still curious.

Hefty Thoughts
Hefty thoughts from an exaggerating teenager
May they all just lose their heads!
Exacerbate every situation, and do not take concern for me

But sweet transitions into upper life
Intrigue more positive states of mind
They calibrate every point of concentration
Until peace and love both cross one plane

You will set aside every problem at your desk
Open your curtains, feel the light, close your eyes
As the light pours in
Place every letter within a bottle, that is in your head, and cast it away

26. <u>Baby Steps</u>

I lost sight of what you had in mind
Absolve my mind of my beliefs on wrong versus right
How I cannot wait to meet you my new munificent friend!
You have given me so much though I have let go of your hand!

I will confront the legitimacy of these fears
          Though it stands to be an awry thing
I will be beneficent and a leader
          So I may be blessed by the truth

I will bolster my pride to allow flooding tears
Even though pride is abundant within my life
I will introvert my heart
Because I believe that is what I need right now

So as this crust within my mind sheds as tears unto the ground
I will give my seemingly invariable life to you
To trade it in for your truth
And I will take those baby steps

Little by little. Inch by inch. I stood at rock's bottom, and I set up my camp. Smoke did too little to be called an SOS. All I did was create cover from those looking down from above. From the north came a great fire! I was in a state of turmoil feeling alone. I was alone. It did not take too long, though comprising more than one percent of life, to realize the only way to go was up. A single step in the right direction led me to my best friend. Some may believe him to be a mythical creature. I assure you he is real. Part Bear, part Cat, and mostly honey.

A chef by nature and the epitome of what a man should be (at least to me). We began to spark light in the darkness. Addiction, betrayal, misinformation, theology and religion as a whole... The philosophy of the Heart of David began to spawn. Physical, Mental, and Social well-being was what we would seek for seven long years. I spent twice as long as a mischievous young lad. At the end of these seven long years we parted ways, and we hope it is temporary.

27. Ankles

Many people now investigate us
But whether dark, pale, or in between
They make up all of my friends
>   Though inside my flesh lived an irascible man
>   I had to calm him down and bring justice unto him
>   Because he needs to fit in
These many colors have catered for my pre-broken heart
Though it brought up many questions like…
Where have you come from?
What do you know?
They want to bring me out as a lying fool!
They want to hang me up
I want to bring justice unto you
>   He then propelled me
Joshua said, "You will achieve some brilliant things!"
So as long as you never give up, you will see
I remember thinking I will never mess around
I remember thinking I will pace myself
>   And place myself upon higher ground
This relevantly relented barren seed
You must place yourself amongst people nothing like you
So I pray, "Lord, hold my ankles tight as I drop in
I am trusting in a friend. Do not let me go
I cannot save this world alone!"

28. Mindset

If you ask a heart how it is doing
It will inquire, "What is your opinion?"
It may be skeptical as to why you intend to express your mindset
So if I seem to be dancing on this notion
Help me become aware of my mindset
>   If I am out of tune
Let me know love
>   If I am drifting towards the moon
Please, let me know love
>   If I came and then went
Would you let me preach to them?
>   If I pleaded to be there scent
Would you let me guide them?
>   My mind is set to love them

There is significance in letting love grow
I hope you hope so
If you stick around I will let it all show
Stay for the show and you will know

29. The Foundations of Earth

I want to be your friend
I want to lose it
       Though losing it is no typical way to be free
       For they will flee
He speaks of free flying birds
And freeloading girls
       Hey says, "Take what you can you half-sized flea
       Then come flee with me."
He begs for that sweetie to take his hand
To run off towards a faraway land
       Do not believe them!
Come now timid one
Come now! Your time has come!
       Yet I can feel you standing near
       I see you not treated fair
       Captivated by silk and linen clothes
       Lost within a web of promises so bold!
God pity!

And so he will take them all down
Every foundation on this earth
America is losing her beautiful shine and her worth
And slavery is still something. Real as the blood on my heart
Monsters and strangers are lurking!

30. Old Man Rodney

Old man Rodney walked down to-wards me
He told me he was leaving
I asked him where he would go
I could see he had little time in his life left for searching
       He said, "Dear friend, It is not like that at all."
Though his body was frail, his mind was still strong
And for every second he had spent his own way
They were all borrowed, so he was giving them back that day

He then rolled away his stone
He said tomorrow it would not be over
He said, "See what I can do!"
Now that more time has gone
The morning just does not seem to be quite as long
And days fly by when your love is true
       So get out of your head!
       The day is young and winter is at an end
       You must dive into the clay
       Then we shall find something nice
       Give away more love for one more lovely night
       Do not worry about what others say
       You will be okay!

Now that you are growing up so fast
There will be many more reasons to keep on keeping on
The world may be changing
But realize you cannot just slow this life thing down
       You must put up with the worst in thee
       I will prove in love so unconditionally
       Never breaking down
       Not a single man can take me down
       For I have turned my life around!

Love is All We Need
I need you
I now see I love you
In the midst of these crazy things I am seeing
Love is all we need
She past the judgment bluntly towards me
I responded, "I must dream before I speak"
But these crazy things still deem
To me... love is all we need

31. Underneath the Fallen

Let us see what he will become
To give a life! To give it all!
        To be a father and a son
And OH! The pain of life he will bare
To do the right thing for his people who seem to not care

There is a choice for him to make
As a virgin birthed a gift for an entire human race
        With stomach pains as none before
He will soon walk for thirty days
He will continue for ten more

And so he will watch as we fall into the one who causes problems
We cannot see that he is hiding underneath the fallen
When I close my eyes to see what is on his mind
I can hear his plan for my whole life
        It is played in symphony as angels sing
        Laud the Lord! Laud the Lord!

32. The Slave Dealer

I have been justified
I am ready to die
So will you please come inside with me?
        I have seen you stalk your prey Satan!
My slave... I have become uncertain
        Should I make you stay?
        Should I just set you free?
Things about me have not changed
I walk through this world and it remains the same
Could I be more like him?
What would this life be without any of them?
        Things about me have not changed
        Therefore
        The Slave Dealer will be my name
But things about me should always change...
Stubborn WOMAN!
        She is giving me something...
Thirty years... I work this land... make my name...
Then she comes out of nowhere fighting
        So beautiful...
        She is stuck in my brain
Things about me should change
Yet the Slave Dealer remains my name
Should I believe to be more than this?
I do believe my life would be great without all of this!

To be a slave dealer in today's world. I doubt it was ever a thing to be proud of... Regardless, I traded my sanity for someone I never should have been. I became a lover of a woman who did not know the Lord. Like Samson, I was tied to the chair and my hair was cut, my strength was stripped from me.

I dream. I am at a library. I see an old couple walking around. The man is patiently waiting as his wife looks for a new book to add to her collection. She walks around and around hoping to find the perfect addition, and he patiently waits in admiration of the woman he fell in love with many years ago. It reminds me of my brother. It reminds me of what I could have if I were not captivated by a desire to save souls. Maybe she is out there waiting for me... Maybe her one desire is to save even more souls than I!

I am a simple carpenter. I am a simple man with big dreams. I am a musician and a poet. I am a writer and a lover of mankind. What is she? What is her name? Does she already exist within these writings? If so, how can the Lord prepare me to recognize her when she comes my way? Will she understand my heart? Will she be able to see my life as a replication of David himself? Of Arthur himself? Will she learn me as the son of David, and will she understand my eagerness to pursue the Heart of David?

I have had many wives, yet I have born no children. I have had many women come and go, yet none stuck around to shuffle through the truly hard times of life. This leaves a void in my soul. It is a void only filled by the Lord himself.

33. The Void

I look around to a world so full of holes
Authentic child will become proud for what he knows
To take a stand and bustle you to help me make a change
To save a girl from a life worthy of complaint
    And as we rise,
    And we will rise towards the surface
    A bond will be made
    There will be no more wandering for a lost trust
So if I shout for you, will you truly hear me?
If I cry out is there a Lord who will truly send thee?
Forever more, if I conform, will you cancel all of it out?
To trade everything in this life, would you let my heart abound?
    For as we rise,
    And we will rise towards the surface
    May the Lord reveal the Eye!
    So we may see what is before us

Everything! Nothing!
They both have their reasons
    Though no one knows why
Every man has his own plan!

If you ask what will happen now
    How do we continue our confluence?
If I continue down this path towards all that is right and wrong
Truth may be the poor man lives freest
But life is far too short so for every moment I must seize it
    Because as we rise,
And we will rise towards the surface
You will see it is we who have made it!

The first song written in inspiration of the girl who took a boy younger than herself. She wanted to give it all to a child. This may not have been the right thing to do, and I am sure that she questions this herself. It is a rare thing. Older women, older women, continues to spin in my head, yet the one who captures my attention at this point in time is but a year younger than myself.

My guidance has led me to believe that the best possible team I could assemble would consist of people who are just shy of my age by a few years, so I could properly be accepted as a mentor. I notice this through my Internship at Southside, I notice this in the formation of my company, the FergusonPoetryProject, and I notice this in my day to day functions as a leader in training.

Maybe when it comes to be the leader of a household I should abide by these same laws. I believe it could be possible to continue pushing forward as long as I have the support needed to push onward. I have consistently been the youngest person in the room up to this point. I am beginning to obtain years under my belt, and I am beginning to be the leader I desired to be at the age of fourteen when Joshua first appeared to me.

The woman to my left and the woman to my right would agree that we are all called to accomplish a certain task. Mine is to dream big and to work hard until the end of my days.

34. A Psycho Dreamer

I am told that she is incapable of feeling
I am told I must dig my own way out of here
I must be patient and grab a hold of the time
I must grab it!

I cannot believe I have lost my heart again
I cannot believe you have found a way home!
I am so very sorry to have lost it... and you
Where were you?

You want me to die
        I want you to go
You want me to get out of your life
        I want you to go
You thought of me dead
        I thought of you a lie
You thought I was timid and shy
        And that is just one big lie

If you care, you never have to lie
Do not be the kind to bite your own tongue and ask me why
To have the audacity to ask me why!

A psycho dreamer told me," Believe in everything less we can see"
She said I was never meant to understand
Her great work or her great plan
This ladylove; I will lift her very high
This lust could rust any man's mind
If you were ever my love, I would forever be weak
For I have fallen upon my knees
For Ishtar, the stranger

      I lost them both. I lost them both. I lost them both. The woman to my left; the woman to my right. I lost them both. Neither were mine to begin with... yet I hurt as if I lost my kin. The one to my right took five men in one night. The one to my left retreated deep into her own self. I lost them both.
      Friends make decisions that hurt themselves. Lovers make decisions that hurt everyone around them. Acquaintances will walk by in shock. But, will you simply walk by, or will you stop to heal the wounded? Will you be different? Will you be patient?

35. <u>Mountainous Air</u>

The tables have all turned
        The floor is now filled with stars
I exist under a broken heart

I feel the wind
        It is circling the room
Just swirling the fumes amidst this hallway surf

"The laser show was off"
        It hurt more to hear you say
"You missed my birthday"

I could not take one day
        Not out of my selfish year
This hurt to hear you say

How am I supposed to breathe?
        Without such mountainous air
Why is it so hard to feel?

        Undress within this smoky mountain top fog
And then slowly start making love

Heavenly Composition
Laud the Lord, King of Kings.
He is a well-bred workingman
He writes sonatas in his dreams
They are about his future family and friends
He awakes before the Lord
Who asks him to play his dreamy song!
Though one sonata lengths eternity
It will take him every day, and all daylong!

We all have a song. This song is the calling. This song is what should drive you every day. I had a dream. In that dream was a song that never ended. Though the dream ended the song still plays in my head. This song will be here with me until my last days, and it will continue long after I am gone. This is the song sang by the angels in unison. This is the song of eternal peace.

36. A Smart Man Knows He is Weak

No sense for scientific scares
No need for arbitrary reason there
      One full proof plan to take us far
      Through answers written in the stars
A smart man who knows he is weak
Will still force the strong unto their knees
      To have a simple need to satisfy
To read a book written for you and I
      Would you cast it far off from the shore?
      Would it keep the minds at bay from war?
A smart man who knows he is weak
Can still force the strong unto their knees

Truths will be covered
Truths can be mean
      They will hide them from the weak
      They will keep them from the meek
But that smart man who knows he is weak
He will force the strong unto their knees

37. My Perfect Home

I have traded sounds with other minds
I have walked tall next to the sacred kind
I have been caught up, wicked, within thorny vines
My eyes were opened within a church of lies
>   I will follow no man into the grave
>   I will walk up along eternal waves
You will come around when the wine is gone
You will need me once your time is done
You will flourish within a field of bones
You will want to walk upright once your legs are lost
>   But I will follow no man into this grave
>   I will rise up along eternal waves
Continue your wrong and you will not live long
You will work your fingers to the bone
You will wish to rest among perfect waves
>   If you do your best with no regrets
>   If you put your free will to the test
>   You will rest watching from the perfect home
>   Let us rest watching from our perfect home!

38. Inside My Home

Am I qualified to ask a couple of questions?
Is it possible to become something,
Other than a represent of anarchy?
Would you say, "Hell NO"?
Is it right for you to tax your own daughter?
Keeping her from going further
>   Than her daddy's expertise
I am heading out and running
Much farther than imagination
I am heading out and running fast
So, all that is left from me is dust
This is what we all will soon be

Can I attempt to be a person outstripping problems?
I will not mimic misbehavior for I will once be old and weak
I will fight for your problems because my television is burning
It is featuring this "*Intoxicating* life" while I sit all alone
If this "happiness" is all around me than it is hiding very well
Inside my Home

39. Lady Maid

We have crossed most every bridge
My lady maid would never confess to this
There must be a way to get out not going out this way
No promise of mine has been kept until today
        They want me to keep to myself
There are better ways of how to live
                Keep to yourself what you teach your own kids
                I am sure mine will turn out all right
Can I come up with any more words to compliment a mother?
A mother who listens to her child is expressive yet innocent
                The answers she seeks are nothing short of truth
                Your questions, my answers, I will give them all to you

Can you see? I live for you
Lady Maid
I will not wait to watch our lives crumble to the ground
I will not wait because I live for my lady maid

40. Snake

The last one standing will go
He wanted her first, so she fled, so only she knows
"The dangers of this snake" she has burned in her head
She alleviates the fear by eating an apple instead
                "Delicious and ripe" as she passes his way
                He agrees for a reason she cannot understand
                He hates every second of the taste, but he put on a face
                Her happiness is all that matters to him
Forgive them, my Lord, for what they do and what they say
They have become lost within the ways of the world
                Our God has let us go in this way
                Everything once known has all changed
As if it is a game

Give me your heart, and I will give you my mind!
Her love and my mind is enough for us to fly!
Then we can fly away from this world and it's all
The suffering, the pain, the Fall!

Take what you will snake
The snake will wait and hide under a rose
Take what you need and flee from your home
                Only with me can you live forever!
The promiscuous snake will seem to wait forever
But will prominently perish for foolish endeavors

Steal Me Away

Feel the sunshine
Feel the warmth
The cool of the nighttime
The mist of the dawn
To hold another like you would be great
Your love, it steals me away

Younger me could not feel for a love so right
Younger me was not bright

The Lord shows mercy
I have carried it a long way
Her love is the horizon forever pushing away
I found again a love just like you
Your puissant love, once again, steals me away

I am questioning the purpose of these writings. Will anyone ever read these words? Will these songs be lost forever? What if I truly begin to shift the focus of this message towards love? What if I only pinpoint the importance of love? What is the Heart of David?

41. Stay Alive

You are expertly sly
     I may have mistaken you for a robber
I did mistake you for a goon
     Shy were you? Were you just coming in for water?
Am I wrong?
     Am I cold?
Do I have filthy hands?
     Did I make matters worse?
It took long, yet I have sold...
     One empty hand for two empty hands!
Two Empty Hands!

Be happy; stay alive
     Do not go into the light
Be happy; stay alive
     Do not let your spirits roll away
Do not let your spirits roll
     Legion

Physical, Mental/Emotional, and Social health are imperative to achieve a state of true bliss, or true spirituality. A perfect balance of these three elements can allow one to access a sense of spirituality otherwise impossible to be accessed by the average man. I have in many forms and in many ways described this philosophy in journals and other writings, but it is time to explain it in deeper context using these numbered "poems" as analytical data.

Throughout the study of these writings you will see a shift from an imbalanced teenager into a young man that is somewhat balanced. This is the closest I will ever be to being a scientist, and I thank Cognitive Science for the desire to create this archive of self-experimentation.

Just like my forefathers I have spent over a decade recording thoughts in the form of poetry. Given a religious foundation as a child I have been in constant witness to the power of recording. My kin can be seen worldwide as being one who has impacted millions through recordings. Also, these messages tend to be all over the map because I was in a constant struggle to find balance. Even with this knowledge I tend to fall out in multiple directions, but I have noticed I quickly find my footing which takes me back to the foundation of love (which is solid as a rock).

42. Years

I do not know what you see from this
I see a wife longing for her husband's kiss
We all look around it
We all seem to doubt it

I want to take what I have not worked for
It is this mistake that will take me from the door
Are you locked outside of my door?
Would you lock me outside of your door?

I do not know what you expect from this
I see a child longing for its mother's kiss
We all look around it
We all seem to doubt this

After all these years
One love, one heart, one fear
Come home and be safe, I swear
You have started all of this through war!

43. No Love Wasted

I thought that my love was wasted on you
Like a ghost passing by a dead man's eye
This will never happen again
Memories of this kind
        I am facing a lost youth
        As a dream lost in the night
        I will step away from indecision
        I will step away with no mind
For love was not wasted on you
It is impossible to do so
Love will happen again
Because it has to
        I will move again
        I will build a new home
        I will stand ground on what I believe
        I will step away if I have indecision
        I will step away if I lose my mind

Forgiveness. True forgiveness is one of the greatest lessons to learn. Coming to terms with change is also a great life lesson to learn at a young age. I am very happy to have gone through everything I have gone through because it has made me who I am today. I am grateful for all of my friends.

44. Around

You fight out too long. You drag things out too long
You will only age and break down
Love will go around, around, around
        It will go and grow for a flower child
        Just the same, the wind will call you by name
        Love will pick you up
        It will spin you around, around, around

If your heart is broken, then you should take your time to heal. Relationships are not something to be rushed into, and before growing intimate with someone physically, mentally, or socially you should know what you are getting yourself in to. I have been listening to a lot of sermons about relationships lately; the most recent was how to stay in love years after the puppy dog phase of falling in love ends. Study unconditional love.

45. Happy-Go-Lucky

You lift me up high
As high as a happy-go-lucky, inflated, floating balloon
What makes you to be so much lighter than the breeze?
What make you, to me, to be utterly consuming?
   Is it because you laugh so hard you stop breathing?
   Is it because you take me so high?
My ears start quaking!
   You have stolen my trance from me
   The origin is unexplainable and exciting at the least
You trip me up and pounce on me
You are way too silky for my earthly being
Our love is many light years away
Yet this love has captured my heart in the now
   I guess it is what you have awakened in me
   It is how you take me past what simple eyes can see
   And I now see so much that is new!
   Things I have previously seen, to me, are now new!

Listen. This morning I woke up after a terribly vivid dream. She was with me once again. It was Halloween. We are walking around the Belmont Campus that sits on the Southside of Nashville, TN. I remember gathering all of my friends together old and new. People that loved me were there, and people that do not love me were there.

The concert began. My love appeared to be perfect in her costume. We ended up laughing ourselves to the floor. We were genuinely happy. The room began spinning and spinning until an alarm began going off. The house was on fire. People were running and screaming. I woke up suddenly in my bed.

Realizing I was going to be late for work I rushed to get inside my car. The same car I would take her out in. My dirty white Nissan Versa that she would willingly get inside. I am dizzy. I am not present. I am hurrying to be on time. I begin to focus my vision and realize that I cannot stop in time. I was so consumed in my own head that my foot had steadily been pressing the accelerator.

Smoke, haze, confusion, and adrenaline was reality as I jumped out of my totaled vehicle and ran to check up on the bystander I just crashed in to. I asked quickly if he or she was alright and an older man came out dressed in a police uniform. He was responding to an accident that had just occurred when I hit him.

And so, he ended up being okay. And so, my car is wrecked and my back is very soar. And so, I attempt to continue on with my day. A few hours later I am still locked in my own mind. I discover an old friend passed away nine months pregnant taking her daughter to Heaven with her. They passed in a car accident because someone was not paying attention. What if my actions were reckless enough to take the life of another? How would I live with myself? I am thankful to be okay. I am grateful to be alive, but I am sick of being reckless. I am sick of being irresponsible. Life is hard and there are plenty of things that will happen beyond my control, but for what is in my control I will control it! I will pray for insight, perseverance, and patience.

As my day closes I am taught one of the most important lessons taught by Mr. Boyd. This is God's Story. This is not the story of mankind. This is not the story of me. This is the story of God and his pursuance of love towards his creation who constantly turns away. This is the story of God. Let my life be simple. Let my life be simply a character that acts as a bridge between mankind and our Father the Creator. Bad things happen to good people. This is life. God does not wish harm on anybody, but it is not in his character to stop all bad things from happening. Love is strange.

Jacob's Ladder
I am pressured to leave now
My spirit is raging me to go
I am to follow the course
Between the Faith of Abraham and the Staff of Moses

46. Hunting

Do you see them feeding with their heads low and shy?
       I hope they will stay and graze more
I love how she adores this cool morning
       I will watch her a little bit more
I will see where her power is born
       Once I pull her in I will soon be walking down
I will walk right up to where God placed his hand
       I will go where God has given breath
I will take it away
That will be her grave

If you can, try to spot them in the field
       I trust our scents will not scare them off
For our scents are heavily masked
       Child
Do not be afraid
       This is how men are made
Let us walk down to where God once gave life
       Let us take it away
To create another grave
       Once at the beginning,
Once at the end of these long days

47. Heading South

I saw a group of homeless men today
Interest swooped up in my head hoping for the estranged
The burdens these men carry are far beyond my head
I lack the strength to save these people
I need some helping hands
       I picked a very strange fight today
       To prove myself a winner on grey versus grey
       Maybe I will learn my lesson and get back in the race
       Or maybe life is not a race at all... I need some space
South I am bound
If I do not figure this life thing out
Abound is my heart with this love
Anyone who wants can get them some
Reflecting on bad decisions strays me from the one
       Apparently if you are heading south
       Lack of awareness will waste you wandering around
       Apparently the wrong way is south
       Would your ancestors be proud?
       Some would cheer for you to head down south

48. I Am America

We found love within an empty space
We grew as one against our age and our race
We will never back down with so much at stake
We are seeds in a field with too much food to yield
      We found this world
      We found this beautiful place
      We made it our home
      We became the greatest
We will never give up when women and children are at stake
May the beautiful rise again as a riot of faith
      I will give you all I have
      Family and Faith
      I will show the world we are made from love
      Not hate
Use soft-spoken words to encourage change
We can break this barrier so any man can be saved
      For I Am America
      I am freedom and love
      Together we lift each other up
      We are America's last hope

If I were to claim religion in a modern world... I would claim my patriotism towards freedom and love and declare that I am an American. Yes, I have been studying the Bible for many years now, but we are not there yet. We still exist in the mind of a teenager. All of these poems... all of these writings... and as I read some of these I find it harder and harder I wrote these or even co-wrote these, but this is truth.

God seemed to be revealing himself to me in strange ways though I was a declared atheist. I declared agnosticism when I thought too hard. I declared hatred when I let my anger and denial get in the way of honesty and loyalty. It took five years of pretending and five years of running to end up on home's farm. It took ten years to end up on Southern Ground while staring across golden fields towards my lover as I blew my saxophone towards the house of communion my father built. I stand on top of these green hills listening to the echo repeat phrases as it bounces off the shining zinc exterior that reflects the sun's light almost as beautifully as it reflects the sound of my brass.

49. <u>God</u>

I did not choose to play this part
God must have a different plan for me
I am just a man and not fit for all of this arguing
Though I can lay it down

I will always give you my best
Alongside my brothers I will give my body to the world
As we leave home it is recognized
Mama and papa cannot help you anymore
No more!

Soon life will be seen as a heavy load
Burdens will come and clear paths will turn foggy
Do not turn the other way!
Long after leaving home you will realize
It is necessary to build a new home

Would your mother's God lift this load?
It seemed when life got to heavy mommy always helped me
She would say,
"A mother to her child is my God to everything!"

When you grow up and leave your family
Will you take these strengths and...
Lead long lost people through the world
Help fill peoples heart with mercy and joy
Help people see light in the brand new days
Help people sign their hearts away
Retrieve your brother's and sister's names!

The river will begin to flow
You will be strong and unafraid
The world will still have its weight
Struggles will beckon for you to lose your love for love one day
Emptiness will attempt to steal away your brain
You may feel you are to fade... but you will not!
For faith is more than biblical
Faith is eternal
When life gets to heavy father will always help thee
For a mother to her child is the Lord to everything!

50. <u>Love, from the Water</u>

I am away from the world in the blue
I would not be so cold as to leave you alone
I am digging out the strength so I can take us both home
You need the best in me and I need your hope
Your faith in me is all I need

Speak for yourself if you think something is not right
There is no other person I would rather live by
I know what is indeed best for me
But I care more deeply about what is best for you
I am figuring out this life thing as I go

Feed me your love and be brave
I am patiently waiting for you
Your current has stolen both of my legs
Swallow me hole in your blue!

I recall a night where I heard a voice. It led me to a place I used to meditate called Pools Mill. I walked down to the playground and across the bridge to where you can begin to hear the water cascading down the flat rock that formed a natural waterslide. "Walk on the water" the voice said.

I paused in disbelief, but the voice grew louder. I took off my shoes, but not my socks. I dipped my foot into the water and could feel the coolness of the water being absorbed into the fabric of my sock. I walked over to the concrete bench that sat beneath the flickering streetlight and began to sing hymns of my childhood. Once again I heard the voice.

I stamped over to the water's edge once again and stepped out onto the rivers surface. As my left foot pressed against the water I could feel the surface tension wanting to keep me up. I knew that if I believed hard enough this water could support me. All I needed was enough faith! I began to raise my other leg and as my body weight was full removed from the solid ground I began to sink into the water.

If only I had more faith...

White as Light

I feel that I have met you before
Your beauty is overwhelming me more and more
Is this same feeling taking you?
Is this truly the perfect time where I will never lose?
I am going to take this chance...
Because I Love You!

Now please, let me learn all of your ways
Let this be a great escape for truth
I can carry you into deeper lands
Placing your hands on my hands will do
So well we will work as one, not two

I love how I feel like I am a kid with you
This time we will remember for the rest of our lives
Now that I feel I am new and not used
Our faces will become...
White as Light!

The forefathers of a royal line have been despondent within their faith. This correlates firmly with the incorrigible acts of judgment they have placed upon their own kind. Your brothers and sisters are becoming more audacious day by day. This will result in rebellion and revolution. I know not right from wrong. I know not the proper way to handle neither buffoonery nor early signs of anarchy. But I do know people. Every man desires to be a part of something and not apart from everything. From this, I will join my brothers in arms to help protect the less fortunate with the best of our abilities. This will be known as a brotherhood in its first generation. The vein of the bible-belt holds a love so vitalized in worship it has become notorious of hosting the greatest music within the world. It is our duty to spread this love and music to less fortunate communities. We feel that it would be most symbolic to begin within the states, specifically Georgia which is the Foundation for the Southern Ground we serve.

More than that... the cleanliness of spirits, the prosperity of a promising economy, a conservation and refuge for nature, and the promise of a better tomorrow lies amidst these hills I once called home. I know this because I witnessed it every day. I see that people are still people; some people are good, and some people are bad. Yet, if we can transmit these wonderful ways of life and love through the rest of America, then we can see the greatest country in the world unite in a way not seen in over one hundred years! It begins and ends with worship. So, now I may ask... What do you worship?

<u>End</u>

PART TWO...
Jacob's Ladder

Opening

Laud the Lord. King of Kings, forever in eternity
Celebrate every day and bless the Lord in this way...
Hold fast to your lover's hand
Turn enemies into dearest friends
Thank your mother you are alive
And thank your father for family pride
Brothers and Sisters in your name
We surrender to Allah this way!

The man on the screen is talking to me again. He makes sense and is respected by Mr. Shelton. I listen intently. I am working steadily and am eager to finish this project at hand. I cannot wait to impact more and more people through the power of music. I am eager to change lives. One by One my brothers and I work to impact one more life. Day by day it is taking its toll as I grow older. I exist on one plane. Jacob's Ladder goes up and up and up. I am starting to hear the angels singing. I believe the louder the sound gets is a sign that my end is coming closer and closer.

No man will know the hour or the day, but we can all agree we are growing closer and closer. I am not ignorant to this. The days are beginning to trickle by faster and faster. The father stares at his son, who is a man, yet he sees his baby. He sees a baby. This is the Will of the Father. We were all babies at one point in time, and I would not be ridiculous to say we are all still babies.

Love is All We Need

Do not curse a loved one on the leave
The sun should never set on a churning mind
Love will be lost unless you believe
You will always yearn to reconcile

Within this crazy life, I believe truly,
Love is all we need
Amidst these crazy things I see, and what spawns in every dream,
Love is all we need

51. <u>So Well (White as Light)</u>

I feel I have met you before
The faith of Jud-Man
Is this the same faith I have known?
He recites scripture as we stand in this magical place
So well we work as one, not two

I already know your ways says the Lord
I can be your great escape says the Lord
I will carry you into deeper lands says the Lord
Start with your hand on my hand says the Lord
I am taking this chance so I can be with you
This time we will remember for the rest of our lives

I feel as though I am a kid with you
Once again, I do feel I am white as light!
Once again, the Lord forgives me

Renditions and confusion is the message of this book. A time in my life where I began to question and study religion. As a teenager I was enraptured by the concept of religion because every person seemed to have one. I wanted to discover which religion was going to be best for me because I knew there was something powerful about it. It was not until I dove down into the depths that I realized religion is the source of most of the world's political torment and distress. Animals rage over whose god is most resourceful, and these practices make me sick.

Allah is the Islamic word for God. Yahweh is the Hebrew word for God meaning, "I Am". Islam does not believe that Jesus is God. Christianity is some sectors believes that Jesus and God are one in the same. The question of, "Is Jesus God?" is what stems the majority of my research, and it is what gives me purpose when studying more about God himself. I feel that God has been revealing himself to me in remarkable ways since I have been asking this question.

I am not one who is for religion though I come across to some as being religious. I love personal philosophy. I deeply admire the philosophy of Christianity. I myself am not a Christian. I have a firm belief in the trinity though I have created my own diagram to make it more logical for myself. By asking people of all walks of life if Jesus is God it breaks the ice (or forces people into immediate defense), so I can get to the deeper roots of what makes that person believe in what he or she believes in.

52. I Would Trade It All

Shame seems to linger in my brain
I feel as though I am alone
Like swinging on a swing
Or standing in the rain

The sunrise seems to be burning holes
My mind feels trapped in this cage
The houses built on sand are falling
So now I question the rock

Grace is lost

Maybe you will be revealed through Crystal's Eye
I miss the river's sweet mouth now that mine is dry
Pull me from this ledge
I feel insane
I may not miss much, but I have shed many tears for you

I would trade all I own for love any day
I may not have much, but for love...
Still, I would trade it all

I fear the Eye for my sake
I have come so far
Let me in
My family is waiting

Romance at an early age can distort the reality of what marriage should be. Romance at an early age can also prepare you for the many hardships that are to come when you enter into your later stages of life. It is so much harder to relate to someone as the years go by because both people get specific in their likes and in their dislikes. It makes choosing a partner near most impossible.

Notes to the younger version of myself can be adequately sold as communicating in the worst of ways. I know the future me is now looking at the present me through memories, yet they can't communicate. What if there was no purpose? What if it was all random? It was so scattered with emotion and shame. The only person to blame for such inconsistency is myself because I was such an inexperienced writer. Even today I am still random and sporadic, but at least now I have purpose. The transformation from fear into confidence is here. The transformation from lost to found is here.

53. Younger Me

They will never understand
They will never see
    How sad is a bird that cannot fly?
I made her cry
She would have done the same
    I wish that I could change
    I hate to break the heart of a gentle dame
It is so sad that the younger me could not feel for a love so right
But then again, Younger me was not bright

We carried along through the streets of Charleston
Nothing seemed to be the same
    I thought I had lost my mind
    I saw stranger mercy within her callused eyes
Younger me could not feel for a love so right
Younger me was not bright

54. Kiss Me

You came from the air and left me nowhere to go
So falling in love as children was foolish, but we did not know
Summer came and us two became insane
I told her forever; her innocence swept her away

I do not think I will miss those days
But since I have met you I do pray more

I am sorry I have to leave
So please kiss me
Kiss me!

    I got to relive a childhood romance that I thought was lost to the currents of time. I got to attempt a relationship that was stripped from me against my will. I was given an opportunity to try out young love, but the timing still was not right. I got myself into a very tricky situation, and all I wanted was to get out. I did some terrible things. I added unnecessary pressure to a woman with a weak back and she broke. I wanted to gather my strength and try again, but I was once again not ready. I cannot believe I was to go as far as to tell her I loved her. Though there was truth in it I still did not know what love was by that point.

55. <u>What is Just?</u>

You may be standing still
But he sees you right there
His mind will turn your fears into silent screams
Do not be broken down
It is up to you to decide in the end what is just

Within my house you will wait and ponder
What can this love offer for someone like me?
I have such burdened hands and a heavily broken heart

It is torn
It has been ripped from my soul
So much that it is shown through my eyes
I will try to let this "love" take hold

I will give you everything I have and more
I will make it easier, but in the end it is you that decides
What is just for your soul?
In your heart, what makes you whole?

Love Cannot Ignore
You got inside and so I drank you like wine
I stumbled to your door and played your game
Now I want more
So much more
You said, "Get up! You are welcomed home!"

A love I can see! For every single little thing!
I promise you will never be ignored
Love cannot ignore!

56. Jazz Choir

Everyone needs that lovely song
That takes your mind to where it belongs.
In a daze...
Like a true jazz choir sing along
I will let those notes choose right from wrong
That is the way
   I know some days I lose my way
   That is just the price we pay
An old war veteran was speaking to me
Explaining how no freedom is free, so they took him away
His neighbor's wife happened to be a survivor of a meth O.D.
A dealer's mistake
   I know some days I may lose my way
   But it has made me who I am today
   And that is okay!

57. Snowman

Rolling around in my poofy red jacket
Rolling bikes down a hill with a wagon attachment
I fought very hard for the big green machine
I gave it all up for true love and my dreams

Let this past melt away like the abominable snowman
His white turned to dirt when the sun came and burnt him
He melted away into puddles at last
Then he ran down the gutters and watered my grass

Water coming from the sky always amuses me; I believe it forever
will. What is not to love about a well arranged lightning shower? Drastic
changes in the weather can trigger my migraines. This intense brain-freeze
comes close to crippling me from daily function. I carry on the day silent
with my entire body aching in pain.

58. Bathsheba

Can you find out what she said about the fall?
The several men who pondered all lost their ways to her
But this is the day I will ponder
        What if she was just lost and crying?
        What if he was pleading for her not to go?
Pickup games will not work for her. They will just not work
Talking about you can be overlearning for two or three
        And there may have been two or three that sent for her
        And so she WAS tempted.
I will not try; I should just go
        "Do Not GO!"

Make your move or step aside
Take a life or you will die tonight
I saw what you had, and so I put it with mine
I watched you die

"I know life can be tough…" he said
"To give everything you have and it never be enough
I know this life is rough
You seemed to have things right when it comes to honor and love

Make your move so I can finish this tonight
I will make you fight for the rest of your life
If your love goes, I will still want you here
Because I need whatever this is!

      Being in a relationship inspired by lust always causes pain. Being in a relationship spawned by earthly desires always results in someone having intense heartbreak. As I socialize with many women I start to realize that I have a lot to offer, yet my head and my heart keep going back to the ones I lost. I go back to one in particular. What is it about her that makes me go back? There is uniqueness in every single soul. I see that uniqueness and become captivated. I see that quality of differentiation and I immediately fall in love despite the known outcome. Is this the love of Jesus or is this the love of the flesh?
      I know that we all have a one of a kind thumbprint when it comes to personality. It is when I recognize what this difference is that I fall in love. Despite the circumstances I will fall in love. This scares me. I want to be a man of integrity, but if I meet a person that reveals a characteristic of God that I have yet to find in another I become infatuated. I become nearly obsessed with the desire to understand this new quality. It is similar to a scientist discovering a new molecule. He wants to understand every facet. He wants to be the one to explain to the world what makes this molecule so fascinating. I find this in people.

I love people so much. Though I find myself hard to bare at times, I am always looking for opportunities to connect with people on an emotional level. It goes deeper. The need to connect with people emotionally and mentally, physically, and socially. There is an essential need to understand people on all fronts because each person possesses a piece of God that I have yet to understand. It is my goal to unveil the Lord piece by piece so I can in turn reflect his light immeasurably.

59. All We Have Done

Do you know about the secret waters we had?
I have held onto so many people of my past
Is it too much to ask for only small things?
For you I give everything!

You have told me to wait for my turn will come
You have brought me time and time again true love
I know it is not easy to watch me
But time will surely bring us together

Is all that I have really done is run in circles?
I thought I was bringing us together or at least closer?

Just gather your people and run for the hills
Rejoice in a future holding peace and harmony
Listen to your heart and follow the course
Gather your people.
Let that be your world charity!

60. Better than it seems

I know you are struggling again
It may feel like this is the end
Take it from me. It is better than it seems!

She leaves when I am lost and feel weak
Just one more time and I will leave
I cannot speak a word or even breathe
She has gone and left me on my knees
        As it may be, it is better than it seems
For nights I lay screaming at my heart
What I need is the one I have lost!
Where would I start? Where should I go?
I am trusting that the heart just knows
        Coming from a dream, it is better than it seems
Four years go around and around
Time is lost and bodies are found
        A grey corner is the past
She moves her hips away for the last time
        Time is a very mean thing
And yet, it is better than it seems
        All of this pressure pushing down on me
Come down!
        Better to believe it is better than it seems

Black Skies

You see the world is ending
It is the fastest movement I have ever seen
Faith in the sun, please come so I can drink you in

Over many cries I hear a crack coming from the sky
The answers slip from me and from you
There is no longer anything to see.
It is all black

If the sun were then to rise up in the east
You would be right next to me
You would be in and around me
For I would be in you

But this shame brings darkening fame to my name
Under the crack remain many cries
They are here to lye for eternity if we remain under black skies

61. Changing Yourself

Infinite space is all around me
       Should I go?
If all of my sorrows could be washed away
       A clean slate
I see a bald girl cry; I see a person die
       Behold a shining light
Another monkey is born
       Another human sings
Can you believe we can fly?

Scream down, scream down little children at me
Feel the fire in your eyes
There is no blood for you to bleed
When you get close to the end you will begin
       Changing yourself
Intimidating spirits drift calmly towards my door
Most of my memories drain away into false earth
A bald girl cries and a person dies
Behold the shining light!
As jasmine bleeds and blooms new seed
       Do you understand that we all die?
       This is the circle of life

I know that when you reach the end of this road
You will begin changing yourself

62. Her Ways

One lost soul sat beneath a tree
With a heart full of love and a mind soon to be
She came up with a way
She wanted to persuade her enemies
If only they could see her better ways

She had a heart so full of love
She opened up and came in for you and me
I woke up!
My head was filled up with love
I had not a word to whisper to my love
   For it was all within her ways

Late for work
Running down a street
Coming down to earth can be the hardest thing
Believe me, when she prays or sings
It is a heavenly thing

I have not a phrase to whisper to my friend
It is all within her ways

Do not worry about repetition. See it as evolution. See it as a resurfacing of an old idea to be merged with a new idea. I am beginning to see things in a new light. I am beginning to reproach sobriety from a new angle. I am beginning to understand the true purpose of existence. I am beginning to see the bigger picture for the first time. All of my efforts and hard work are beginning to form me into the man I have been striving to become and this is a very exciting time. This is an excellent time to be alive. This is an excellent time to evangelize and seek the glory of the Lord. This is an amazing time to be able to worship, pray, fast, and love.

Mother, she has a feeling. She has a sixth sense. She has an awareness unlike most. She sees her as being a perfect fit, and she wants me to keep my mind open and my eyes alert. She wants me to be patient and to work hard. I am listening. I am waiting. I am working hard. I am attempting patience. I am watering and tending my heart's garden. I am taking care of the seeds I have sown and am shooing the birds that attempt to harvest my crop prematurely. I am continuing to worship and write for the people I love and for the people who love me. I am bringing it all together little by little.

63. <u>Stand Up!</u>

This crimson blood was spilled
        Not for you or for me
Same as the tears they shed
        Not for you or for me
This begs me to seek the how and the why

The voice says, "Look up to the starry sky...
Do you not see why?"

Every answer seems to make the sky a bit brighter
It is just as beautiful as the darkness that lies beneath
I wish to be a hero amidst my brothers in the sky
To join the constellations "you and I"

Ancestors call me through the songs we sing
        They say, "We are not so different you and I"
Though I may refuse to believe
        I feel this is not right
Try again the voice says
        You will find a friend to help you towards the end
Come along with me!
Stand up! Watch the world for me. Watch over the world with me.

64. Hold On Sweet

Escape your fate. Lie and wait
I can hear your rusted hands playing the same old damn songs
Did you write that one about that one you lost?
Though you left her...
You mourn as if she is the one who broke your heart

He comes back. He will always come back
He wants to try and take again!
What to me is mine!
Yet, something in you wants to give him a chance
You fool!
There is a better side
        I can love you right
        I can give you the greatest fucking life!
Hold on my sweet
        I will take you in with all of your ways
I will break within. I will lose some friends
But I will not change
        I will not stand for the ones who take and take
They are trying to take my one last chance to be with her
        And I will not stand for a cheating man
        You are worthless and have lost your chance!
Hold on. Please hold on sweet. I will take you in...
        With all of your ways

65. One More Thing

One thing I need my child to know
Before I leave this earth
Understand... all words are meant to help
And NOT to hurt

I, Your Son

You stepped onto our plane
Perfection you became
And then you found a wonderful way out
None can speak nor save
Without your loving grace
So how can I express that I, your son, am proud

66. River Runs

Who knows about these footprints?
They go down to where the river runs
When they stop, so will we
Then we both will start to preach

Go out and please me
Be the one who made me
Sacrifice your wants for your needs
Where the river runs

A long time I have been unseen
We have now filled this earth and have lost our meanings
In the end you will win
It will start where the river runs

Now, back to these secret waters we have
Four men, to hold the people of our past
Is it too much to ask for only small things?
For you I will give everything

That night has replayed in my mind so many times now that it is
starting to appears as rough film lost through time. Fragments remain, and
it will take many men many hours to piece together the remnants. But, what
will they pull from these remaining scenes. Does one fill in the blanks or
take the leftovers for what they are worth? Do people simply pretend to
know the true meaning? Do they believe their own lies?

If I told you that I walked on water would you believe me? If I told
you I felt the surface tension under my feet and that it was almost enough to
hold my hold body weight would you believe me?

67. One Void

You have told me to wait for my turn will come
You have brought me time and time again true love
I know this is not easy for you to watch
I cannot wait for the time when you bring it all together

Look around your room
Look around your heart
Stand up and make a change
Save the people who lack wants
        For they have the most need

How can I do anything?
        I am too small
I have yet to meet a soul who represents you justly
Truth may be you have pushed everyone away
That is okay
        Community is a hell of a vein

68. To the Grave

For years I have lay many nights awake
This ghost of you will follow me into the grave
It is not the same kissing strange lips at night
I am in the dark because you were my light

69. I Am Coming

I have traveled many miles hoping I would find you
You cannot be gone forever! These memories substitute for now
I am searching for just one; this is not a life to live without love
I am sitting on a step. She walks by. I think, "Maybe next time"

I know she is waiting
        It is too hard to open up
I want her to know when I am coming

I need romance
I feel I finally have her in my hands
Does she want more of what is mine?
To become one flesh... one more time

I want her to know when I am coming
And I am coming soon

70. Average People

I woke up this morning
I dreamed a dream most different
I reflected within my mind
I had seen a place more beautiful than heaven
I was there for a while
      At first, I saw people in white claiming paradise
      It was paradise
      I heard my name being called
      I called back,
      "Who are you all?"
They sang to me, "We are not your average people
We have lived here for a while
Now come and pray upon this steeple
Become a newborn child."
      We could live forever
      More peaceful than glassy water
      Everything fine
      But one-day chaos came
      He took them all away
      Tears fell through the night
      I was angry, mad and sad
      I wanted revenge; I wanted that life back
      I thought, "What should I do?"
      The only color left was blue
      Chaos spoke, "Do what I tell you"
I told him I am not an average man
I have lived here for a while and this is my steeple
"You are not welcome malicious child!"
      I awoke in my bed
      I was alone, yet I felt I was reunited with everyone
All of the folks in white were with me.
I felt courage. I felt new. I was confused, yet I felt new

Impetuous

A lack of communication is driving me insane
In every direction there is a flaw
I hear everyone is imperfect
How?
If we are made in the image of God,
Then we should be perfect
I see my fellow man as a perfect creation
I saw a man crippled in a wheel chair
I thought, "There is a beautiful man"
I saw a blind girl
I thought, "She sees clearer than I"
We are all perfect in our own way
Humans are examples of evolution and perfection
But I do not stop there
I see the sky and stars and trees and I feel the breeze of summer
All perfect!
Rainy days, hot days, cold days and snowy days
All perfect!
I am having impetuous thoughts
I want to leave
I want to disappear
They all believe they are imperfect.
I do not
I refuse to believe this
We are all different
But still perfect
I want to go into the world
I want to go into its belly
I want to see what my father sees
Perfection!
I attempt to live every day as if it is my last
I do not want to let my brothers down
But they are sad!
The lot of them
I am not sad
Only when I see dreams burning, and love dying, do I cry
Other than that, I am a smile
I am love
I love too much I believe
I am having impetuous thoughts and desires
I have good addictions and bad addictions
But still perfect
I am lost in the ways of the world
Why?
It is because I will worship
It is because the sun does not set on my head without me thanking God
It is because I am cursed with a heart of longing... impetuously

71. The Servant

The servant serves
He will ask you what you want
He will retrieve it
He will ask you if there is anything else
He will obtain it
This will not be enough
Your glass is half empty
He will fill it back up
Your glass is half full
He will bring you a full glass
He will not charge you for the water you drink
He will quench your thirst for free!

He will smile and tell you to have a great day
This will not be enough
He will bring you bread for free
This will not be enough
He will wake up early and present himself
This will not be enough
He will go to bed later to satisfy your needs
This will not be enough
He will give and give until his last breath
This will not be enough

You demand another servant to take his place
One who does not stammer as much?
One who dreams less?
One who does not ask as many questions?

As for me...
I dreamed a dream in time gone by
I dreamed of men in black
I dreamed those men would change the world
I dreamed their dreams would come true
I dreamed these men would never die
I dreamed these men could never die
I dreamed these men would never stop asking questions
I dreamed these men would be accepted
I dreamed these men would fight for love
I dreamed these men could carry the weight of their loved ones
I dreamed these men could pay the bills
I dreamed these men would encourage free will
I dreamed these men would take on all evil
And in that evil be taken, and in that evil would overcome
Because of love and because of truth

72. <u>Take It Far Away</u>

With a stature he stood to take the blame upon himself
Truth may be told that no one knows
He may just want it all for his greedy little self

He took it far away
Now it has become too much thought for a single day
No lover's touch could make him stay
Let him go out on his own

I rationalize love to myself
I have concluded there is neither heaven nor a hell
I will not let my faith get in the way of what I witness every day

I will take this far away
All of these thoughts every single day
If no lover's touch could make him stay
Maybe I cannot find it on my own

This present state of mind has me meditating
I am attempting not to look too far ahead so I am not as old
Be that as it may... your gods are lost until judgment day
My God is gone until another day

73. <u>Awake My Old Friend</u>

Awake my old friend
Your time in this castle is done
Completely and forever
I thought you would prefer the blessing of becoming eternal
Stoned ladies pray for me
I see your mind is more open clearly
We will not dispose of our loose change
Our company declares it shall not be done

We have all been stained by flesh
This is why she has stayed within these walls
She is the one who can talk to the sky
She will now live forever
She was not enraptured by silk lies
She was only clothed in the finest of fine
Comfortable linens
Linen has tied us all together

Her days quickly turned into years
Her movements became blurs
Impetuous decisions will let her live-forever

74. Trade Me

Stop right there and sway
Lay right here and stay
Do you feel that I have found my place?
It is far from meditating on a rock

If only I could ask myself about whom I am
I believe I would be somebody else
I feel that this is a nice place
You should try meditating on rocks

Trade me back the love I gave you
Trade me. This man in sackcloth
I gave it all, and then broke

75. Point to Make

Sirens blaze, they need to take this new heart
People are living longer these days
I feel I am kept in the dark
So for my own sake, and not heaven's sake
I have a point to make

Lonely days, we have grown apart
I will take a very sharp knife to carve out this corroded heart
For my own sake to leave things this way
It may be strange, but I have a point to make

"Be calm!"
Words I have never heard before
Be strong,
the master is looking through your door

My soul mate has pushed me way too far
Times are a changing, and I am going to be a part
For our own sake, I must end it today
Dear Love, my apologies for this point to make

Houses

I have lived in a pretty house
I witnessed corporate America stamped by a mouse
I have lived in an ugly house
Good cities and bad towns
I have been made of money and I have been homeless
Strung out on drugs with the useless
I have been in limbo and have been titled Jimbo
Now, I play for fun.
I once played for cash, but hard work pays more. In the long run

76. No One

There is this dream I have
It raises me up into the clouds
A voice says, "Watch!"
All color fades away along with any sound

There are people high and people down below
I see them screaming, but I have yet to hear a sound
Not a single question could be asked
For no one could see that blood was raining down

And the world felt as if it was dying
People crying, blood all around
Mistakes made, people dying
No one cares because no one is around

So I take this far away
So many thoughts within a day
I am just a man finding his way
Within a crowd of little faith

77. Looking Down

> I have been pretty busy now
> One whole year has gone by
> I need to get back to my roots
> When summer comes by I am soaring high
>
> Your face seems so much smaller up here
> I am now seeing curves on you I have not seen before
> Yet, I have never felt so close to you
> I am only rising and rising up
>
> I have to pull and tug to stay high
> Voices say do not do it, do not do it, do not do it
> I have to fight for what is right in this life
> I must do it
>
> I feel so much better when I get up and out
> I want to show these things off to my friends
> I know you love me doing this
> You love me rising up
>
> There are people in planes up here with me
> And we are all looking down

An important part of my life has come and gone. A simple memory remains. I am studying the Bible now. I start from the beginning with my mind open. People claim that this book is living and breathing. People claim that the story being told is life changing. I am listening to my teachers that the Lord presents in my life and I find some things that I agree with and I find many things I disagree with, I love some, and I highly dislike others.

Luckily, I have had incredible teacher who I believe to have been sent by God into my life. This is not to discredit any of the bad teachers I have had because the man to my right claims him to be the best teacher he has ever had. I just did not connect. I am now being enlightened. The difference is that the man to my left is also being enlightened. I am not better than him for we see the same thing. Neither of us is better than the man to my right because he was enlightened yesterday. The man behind me will be enlightened tomorrow.

78. I Have Already Gone

We thought the problem was all me
Oh, we were wrong about that
Take what you will
You have concealed
Emotions beyond my turned back
Go and find yourself a new man
One who will treat you really well
There is no more room in here
There are no more frontiers
My building is under attack

You must go and find a new home
This one has lost its foundation
I cannot let you in
I have already gone

The shadow lady will help thee
She helped me forget my troubled mind and past
I have paid her worth since it has worked
The last thing you want is her coming back!

I want to run far from where you are
Forget all the problems and all you have harmed
Up to the Jordan, crossing the line
From what was witnessed to what was left behind
You have known me up until today
Now I say,

"I want to run far away from me
I want to climb up until you cannot see me
I have to let it ring
I am broken and weak. A sinner so meek
Forgive me"

Love found, and love lost. I began writing a book of hymns. A random collection of worship. A random collection. I began and I continue this work as the foundation of all other works. I know this may not make sense, but watch as the chaos turns into art. Watch as the darkness turns into light. Watch as the selfish man figures out how to live a selfless life. I want to run, but the Lord is constantly whispering in my ear, "Stay here for now."

79. My Genes

I see you want up in this bed
It is you with I
Promiscuous, I sense your blood craving mine
Let us leave this all behind
Let us be removed from this society
We push and shove to make our point
We fornicate and print to prove apparent love
You better believe I will not sleep when you leave
I abused the love you spent on me

Some say diamonds are the only way to break through skin
You bought a ring for the wrong human friend!
This you should know for it was written for you and I
True love has no cost; there are no diamonds worth her love

A picnic table is a preference for me
Outside and under the sun is where I want to get hot
I will worship your sun god if it means I can have your love
This is wrong you should know
A gentle scream is music to my yearning ears
A perfect harmony of hums makes me feel real
I will go down
Make me king of take me right now town

Another round?
Silly little girl
I will flip you inside out
I will intoxicate you
These are my genes

80. A Mother

Let these honest dreams help you
Life lived right will be full of happy times
But the darkness will come
Do not worry about the little things
  Find the place where you belong
  You can be as clean as light
Out of the darkness I came
With the power of love coursing through my veins
My people will dance, and our sirens will blaze
All of the lost will come to give this love a chance
  Choked by the brutal chord of pain
  The unholy cage swallowed me
  I laughed as unaware as a child who "cares"
  I was pushed into this life

Playing is Fun

Playing is fun; I do not play for work anymore
The kid in me lives
But he only lives through faith
I looked in the mirror and saw a man
And so time is not broken ha-ha
The flesh will wither
Soon I will be very weak
I have been enjoying my health and my strength
The kid in me remains eternal
Something that time cannot kill; to me that is beautiful
I pity the wealthy man
Buying his happiness
He ages and will not carry his wealth with him
He will never be able to play for fun
Unless he returns all that is not his to begin with
Unless he has strong faith

81. The Knowledge of Love

I am again in disbelief
It is hard to stand on this soil
I want to fall to my knees
I must continue to stand and serve
When they come I will welcome them
But for now I am preparing the feast
I must be presentable for the few
I will only have a few within this life
They will come with me
They must come with me
Heaven is not Heaven without them
They seek to fill their bodies with emptiness
I will fill their bodies with much more
Much more than artificial fuels and sugars
I will fill them with the knowledge of LOVE
      This weapon is more powerful than any other known

I will cut the cord myself
      I have been patient long enough
CHAOS, my enemy
      The lack of self-awareness, hardened hearts
Evil
      False promises and internal hatred
Love will clean these slates stained by evil mortar
A keen eye full of love can fix the faults made by the foolish.
      A clean slate... sounds nice

My wife, I am patiently waiting for you. I do not know you. We may never be together in this world, but we will meet in this world. We will love each other unconditionally in this world regardless if we physically can be together. This is okay because we have an eternity to dance with one another. We will have an eternity to make love in our own way. Let us continuing saving souls.

82. Unless

Begin working towards a dream
Unless you are lazy
Begin thinking about your future family
Unless you do not want one
Go and hangout with the homeless
Unless you are afraid of them
Put your faith in God
Unless you are agnostic
      Work hard
      Unless you do not want to
Let your inner child live
Unless he is evil
Let God Be God
Unless Allah is not God
      Believe man is God
There have been Judges and Kings and Priests and Popes
There have been Presidents and Dictators. Can man be God?

83. And So I Serve

What will you say to make them stay?
      For that extra second, that extra smile
What would you do to connect with a stranger?
      Would you lie? Would you bare false witness?
Would you denounce the foundation of your core values?
      Do you not see who loves you?
Regardless of...
What you say, who you say you are, who you talk to
      I am love unconditionally. And so I serve

84. Memory #1

I remember being poor
I remember a dozen pizzas
I remember everyone filling his or her bellies every night
I remember being asked why I am so poor
I remember going to eat with friends
I remember them not letting me get anything
I remember them asking me why I brought no money
I remember not feeling welcomed
      I realized why we were poor

I am continuing to study the bible. I am studying history as a whole and though the bible reflects the beginnings of Israel and the Hebrew peoples the bible is far more than historical record. The Bible is the story of God in constant outreach to humanity. The difference between the Bible and every other book is the purpose. Just as I write the song, poems, stories, and brief excerpts, I do not want to take away from the glory of God. I have looked at what made the Bible so wonderful. I read the writing of David and Solomon.

I read the writings of these great people who came before us and I notice that the writings that truly stood the test of time were those writings spawned from love and selflessness. They were spawned by a desire for change. The goal for us as a people is to determine what we mean by change.

85. Come On

Come on little mama I will show you how I rock this cage all night
Follow me in between these narrow lines
I know I am second only to your master
And I know he is the one who brought us here
And I know his love is one of a kind
Do you see how I have changed?

Indeed, A Seed
All you know started as a seed
It grew and soon made other seeds
Then all was crushed by a great stampede
All that was left were three bad seeds

All you know started as a seed
And it will grow into a tree of greed
It blocks the sun with its massive leaves
And it kills everything beneath the tree

And so all you are is one big disease
You grew and grew and destroyed the peace
You could make a million doors out of this tree
If only we destroyed the worst bad seed
Even though a bad seed is a seed indeed
There is one of three that is an evil breed

86. I Would Love to Sit

Please allow me to further explain
The Lord should be a cornerstone within this world's society
If you want to back down before it is too late I will understand
Intimidation is a factor to not mislead
       Maybe we should kneel and pray
       Take this fear up, up, and away!
       Maybe we should pray through the night
       Then we can heavily relax through our days
Oh, how I would love to sit and watch you all of the time
But I am up here, and you are down there
If you focus for a long enough second you will realize
       Shade
       The best way to conceal your innocence
       Warmer weather contains a powerful experience
           If you would let it
Maybe I should kneel and pray
Pray you would take this fear up, up and away
I want to love you every second of my life
Give in to me so we can go until the moon leaves the knighted sky

87. A Lit Candle

A laugh to shake the awkwardness
A smile between your ears and amongst your lips
Waking up in view of the grandest wish
Feelings for you are just like this
       I am everyday as you when you are lit
       Standing side by side the same way on the list
       Do you remember the tunnel song?
I bought a gift to lift your brow
A gift so you would pop up to the clouds
And when that doggy pet licks her a kiss
A crazy girl will get her wish
       I am all of the days
       You are only lit
       We stand side by side
       And I sing the tunnel song as my mind goes gone

88. Trust in Me

I would sail across the ocean, but never admit I was wrong
I would reap and sew and orchard, but not admit I was wrong
I would concert an impression before I admit I am wrong
I would fool you to believe I am Cupid and cannot be wrong
      Though we could just get along
      I think it is funny how time steals us
I would take you out of wedlock, and it would not be wrong
I could hold up marches for freedom, and it would not be wrong
Why are the kids no longer funny in this generation?
One million believe they are right and not one could be wrong?
      Trust in me
      Time will tell
      I will not steal from you again
      Let me buy you new furniture
      I will help you
      You do not have to be alone
      I was wrong
Until you I was living under ground
You had me speaking in tongues convincing me to love
I cannot believe you made me think I was wrong

     The rain is falling today at a rapid pace. These songs begin to punch me in the face. I can hear these melodies racing through my head. I begin brushing up on the book of Joshua. I relate this to the Joshua I met. The book of Joshua right after Moses. This is the beginning of the Canaanite Massacre. Joshua is a new Moses. Joshua becomes a new leader for the people. Is time truly beginning to go in reverse?

89. Waste Away

I will call upon you when you share me
Be a part of me, or fall apart
They have a bounty on your head
Cry for free or waste away
      Baking takes time along with being high
      Bring me up into you so I may fuse
      I feel as you did last summer
Heartbroken as you were
She tells those days as no other
Bear naked and unashamed
      I wrote a letter too many days ago
      In the trash it went to reach the whore
      They now share bounty for her head
      Cry for free or waste away
For I will shake this damn place down

90. This Child Is Mine

You cannot deny nor try to hide
You are all alone and it is your damn problem
A feeling you do not know; you cannot let it go
It remains inside
Your mother does not know so she would say just let it go
But it is deep inside

Move out of your home with some guy you barely know
It is all right to have a lover for those cold nights
Words lead to fights
He cannot handle his own life so he flies
You sit there all alone with nothing to call your own
But these lies

She cries at her pitiful life
A kick knocks her down and she feels inside
        It is in you
        It is in me
The power of life and the urge to need
We will all fall upwards towards the sky
Hear the shout from God, "This Child Is Mine!"

Memory #2

Almost as déjà vu puts you in a particular mood
So does the memory of seeing you
Almost as the lengthening shadows foreshadows the moon
So does the tide pull for big and blue
The eye has been watching and lives the long day
Just as my heart beats tomorrow to play

91. Wishing A Way (The Rest of Your Life)

Fortify. Justify
Build up many walls to hide behind your lies
I have tried to reach down deep inside
You keep telling me I am one of a kind
          Will I be only searching for the rest of my life?
My, oh my, is this one really mine?
I look behind myself to see them in a line
With this one chance I will grab your hand
I can prove to you I am a better man
          You will not be searching for the rest of your life
I want to have you crawling over me
If you agree we should all pack up and leave
I want to have you creeping under my skin
I am wishing a way to see this wonder from within
          But I will not be searching for the rest of your life
Sleep nice in your bed tonight
I will keep within my head a big surprise
Lay still and soon we will feel real
I will show you who remain the bigger deal
          They do not have to wonder for the rest of their lives!
          They will not have to wonder for the rest of their lives

92. Memory #3

I carried her down the basement stairs
We fell upon Grand pappy's chair
It was a one of a kind
          Just as she was
It was enough to have her steal
And now she will be forever in my mind

I was heavily stubborn and impaired
A challenging conversation I would fear
She played every tear

I bruise just like a human
I hurt just like a human

These memories terrorize my soul
          I try to let it go
Some memories are enough to swallow me whole
          And so I try every day to let them go

93. Home's Farm

In my head I will be the one to carry you into the sun
I will sacrifice my pride if love does see me through
Majorities of people show their weaknesses
To let you know their hearts have holes that cannot grow
Unless there are you
   Sometimes life is not fair
   That is why we hide behind our Nana B's chair
I know it is not right to keep you waiting every night my love
You need to see me true
All I am and everything, I will give to you
   And when you hide I only see you in light
   No shame will take your hand
   I will guide you out of the dark
   This road you are on will take you to home's farm

94. Loon

It will be hard to sleep outside
The moon is way too bright
It is asking me to dance with it
There is not enough darkness to cleanse my head
There are plenty of people for one large bed
You better believe this is where I am meant to be
   What is so close is so far away
   Could a figment fill this empty space?
   Could all of my dreams escape the make-believe?
   Maybe if an unwanted bird flew my way
I want to snap it down with one good shake
Do you not understand every bird belongs to me?

I may be smaller than the moon but I am lucky and crazy
I am a loon
I just want to rest in peace
Reflect this light and guide me through the night
Because I am wasted and so gone

  This song has been played to hundreds of people. As I retreat to
the mountains I grew up in I consider all of the time well spent in love.
There are many things that I wish I could change, yet I find peace in who I
am. Constant growth has put me on a road only few behold.

95. <u>Celebrate!</u>

Hello old friend
       It is time to ride the currents of the wind
       Take a chance so we may wind up hand and hand
       I thought you were another born with desires as I am
       I am glad you had something to offer I had not yet had
Hello again
       My Lord of love has guided me to this end
       One battle of rage will take place
       We will wind up face to face
       I thought you were another born like me
       I am so glad you were not so now my mind can see
Today is a day to celebrate all we have had
Man-made landscapes for us to enjoy
We should better love this world!

A Funny Guide

I want to leave this mind
I want to escape
I want to believe in your God
But what is yours shan't be mine
I had a guide
It left me to wonder
It left me to wander
And it left me to guide her

96. I am. I am

I have come so damn close to finding you in my own ways
I could not let her take me for I am afraid I would not be the same
But the voice of the deep says to be all I can be
Echoing is another voice mashed by the shackles on its feet
       This road, I feel, I must travel alone
       Though I know I am never alone
Try to freeze the moment wishing some nights would never end
Understand mere mortals have to be a part of sin
And again that voice of the deep reminds me to be me
Long has gone that kid. There is a man to replace the weak
       This road, I feel, I must travel alone
       Though I know I am never alone
Red and blue are blisters upon my feet from walking far
I would walk my feet off just to be where you are
Oh so weak are my knees from jumping off of things
Creepy crawling tricks have made my heart sink

I feel the whole weight of this world upon my head
Could you lift it off before I am gone? Before I am dead?
Could we leave this trash behind so we can rest?
I am right side up I believe I am. I am

97. The Truth

Come inside
       It is very cold
We are all scared of what we do not know
       I am too slow to stay here with you
I must go to find the truth

They say the truth
       When it calls your name,
It is something you cannot hide
       You will see this new life hanging
Right in front of your eyes
       If you take it
Everything you will understand
       Carry onward my brothers
And help your neighbors when you can

We shake up everything we know
       We cannot be anymore
It will be all right as life goes on
       A simple line can take you home

98. Like A Glove

I can patiently wait the rest of the time required
I no longer stay outside during the night
I used to not face myself
I would refuse to look in the mirror until she came home
       I shake off loose ends
       I pray every night
       I pray we will be all right
       I was never one to pray
But when my head got so twisted
It became the only way
       To deal with weight
       To deal with the stresses of this world
The summer gives me gifts of light
And right as it fades
       I notice my loved one's hairs are grey
This lady will take my soul and dangle it above
She will laugh with it and love it and where it likes a glove

99. Little Mama

Once again I drive towards my little mama
In Ole Joe
White Ford
Pick-up truck
Down the road with not even a shirt on
This could be me
Aged
Long white hair
More in love today than when we first met
When I lay eyes on her for the first time
Every day since when I catch her glance
It is even better than that first time
When we make love tonight
It will be better than the first time

100. Green and White

> I am flying out of this world
> Lift me into a newer sky full of green and white
> > Take me out of the darkness again
> > Power and strength coursing through my veins
> > People dance as sirens blare
> > The lost may give this sweet love a chance
> I formed of dust and then spread out
> I then grew a voice; then got loud
> I screamed for a while, innocent as a child
> Reaching and stretching towards clouds
> > Of green and white
> The green is so much greener. The light is so much whiter.
> Let this new sky take you and you may fade into everything

And so, I continue to climb this ladder. I have yet to name it. All I can do is climb it. All I can do is live and love, and take the time to listen. I am searching for an opportunity to help me reach outside of Nashville. This city has hosted my people for a long time now. This city, founded three short years after the United States was born, is the perfect place for my family. We thrive here! Sadly, there is much more to this world than Tennessee. Georgia raised me and Tennessee welcomed me. California will praise me as I journey across the country towards it. Just as pioneers did it during the gold rush from Dahlonega to Sutter's Mill and San Francisco, I will journey and teach the Course of Abraham. My goal is to touch the lives of the travelers along the way. If the window is open the breeze will find its way. I pray I make it back to my love. I pray she is patient and strong. I pray she leans towards you my Lord in times of weakness and sorrow, so that you may make her strong. She has the power of a lioness that I see every day, yet she is as gentle and carrying as the wing of a butterfly. Give her strength my Lord. This journey will be long. And it is all for you. Everything, and all things, should be for you.

Next Class
Moving on
It can be harder than you would realize
I have been writing more than ever
I have been loving every single day
I will forever remember each child's face

My sweet tooth is stronger than ever
I am falling in love every day
A new woman, a new face
I am chasing things, worthless memories

101. The Art of Flight

I say hey to every single feathered friend
      I say, "It is great to see you up on this hill!"
I must sneak all the way up and chase them down
      Yesterday, that was the day to end
There is no day like today to begin the race
      I am racing towards a northern town
They say it has a perfect view when looking down

It is the place where many dreams come to play
      It has been so much fun to write with you today
A story that writes itself if you have been found
      It is a perfect view up here when looking down

From this mountain I see amber skies casting towards the night
I stare towards starry seas in awe of everything
      I am in awe of this life
I cannot believe I came up here just to chase geese
      As If I was doing the art of flight

Come watch the sunrise up to the east and feel the light
      Feel the light!
I hang my hat right here on this limb
      It has become a trail for any fellow man
Seeking to see what is all around
      The perfect view up here when looking down!

102. The Path Our Fathers Laid

I am a man of constitution in a land that has been bought and sold
        A land, which we stole,
In which the votes decide what is "gold"
I am a man of very poor planning
        Procrastination is my downfall
A problem our forefathers saw

I stand and look back at whom I am and what I have got
        I say, "We are a lucky melting pot"
Come here friend
        Take a stand
Let us walk these broken roads hand in hand
        Let us talk about what will become of future man
First, I must travel the path our fathers laid
        To make their dreams real for a brighter day
Come now, it is your turn, you can always learn
        Move that stone; together we will change this world

103. Memory #4

I am swinging
I am looking up at her
This woman keeps me alive
Am I alive?
        What is this?
This world is very strange
        Very different than what I remember
Though I do not remember anything
        Nothing of substance at least
I do recall peace
        But these thoughts escape me daily
I am swinging
I am looking
I am listening and learning so much
I am also forgetting you
I am also forgetting you

104. Johns Creek

In my hometown I am feeling very lost
An hour passes and I have been walking around and around
There goes her house again
Followed by the snake's house again
      Down this corner the flashes will come strong
I hear voices screaming, "Stop!"
They want to know where I am going and where I have been
I have a hammer in hand and my mother would not allow this
      So I ran!
My stomach hurt when in the morning appeared a busted curb

I learned to disrespect you
      Way before the day I learned to take a breath
      And turn the other way
Do you think I am ready to return to this place?
I do not participate nor demonstrate obtrusive thoughts
      Nor do I have abusive tastes
I am hard to love and partial to hate
I am partial towards western morals
      I am free to walk and talk my name

I am cracking up
I am lifting this world off me with no fear
I swear sometimes I am drifting into the air
Floating up never to return. I am drifting slowly, way out there

105. In Every Single Way

Going out. Going back to the hill tonight
The moon is out; every star is bright
What are we in for to play?
I am so surprised to find everyone so high
I understand how the artist is wise
I can understand how we came into this place

My heart is racing and I cannot tell up from down
That is okay
There is so much love here to go around
This lake seems like a great place to stay

We are staying out past midnight
We are rolling in the clay
Same as before, yet better
In every single way!

A Smiling Yellow Balloon
We left some items for you
We left the money to buy them as well
Enjoy this gift today
A yellow balloon for a dark grey day
I bought a ticket for you too
It is for your favorite show
Every word you will know
You and I and me should go

You wore that yellow dress
I remember too vividly
I will never let this go
Something my mind does not want, yet my heart loves it dearly
The yellow is too help remember what I let go
The sun's light triggers this
Yellow is a color no man should miss
Knowledge even a colorblind man holds

106. Apple Creek (Queen of Quirks)

I wanted to fly like birdman
I wanted to flap my wings for my friends
            I would bring them apples from Apple Creek
Boy, my head spins in this coffin
She left me swearing and kneeling

Now I am dancing, dancing
I am feeling rage and courage
Sweat pouring, laughing
I am feeling sweet

She is young, tasty
My body is soar, and she is quirky
I feel nervous as is I am caught in her beam
She has me steady. I love her head in wedding
I think I am breaking down mentally

We should prepare more often
What is at stake is more than you can see
You are smart. You should think it around
I am full of this love; I want to give you loving

I do not want to be sitting here all of the time
My body is sore I am searching for my queen of quirky
I do not want to only be writing all of the time
I yearn to see the world and to feel it
My brain is sore and I yearn for my queen of quirky

107. Men Who Fish

The first followers knew patience
More than I will ever have to know
I was born a farmer and can build a great fence
My parents held a garden where bad weeds did grow
     I met fisherman who was an older man
He gave me guidance and lent his daughter for me to love
     He then gave me another thing he made
A fishing pole
     He told me, "Men who fish can live forever,
Patience is the key,
     Strong faith is the strongest pleasure,
Love is a gift for you and me."
Why choose of fisherman to do the work of the almighty?
Is it because he knows a hard day's work?
Is it because he is willing to get dirty?
I would like to be a fisher of men. That is my endeavor

108. Soon to be...

I woke to singing birds and the rising sun
My lover whispers words and I know she is the one
Our bag is filled with apples. Some bitter and some sweet
My love she loves to travel, but there are children she must teach

They will give her many apples, but of a different kind
So innocent and foolish, but my love will never mind
One day an apple will come and take my wife
I will want to blame the children being overwhelmed with pride

She will be older, yet still full of hope and full of life
My head is not my father's, so I may sleep when I am to die
Though I am grateful for anything and everything soon to come
I long to see the look on her face when our child is in her arms

109. One Penny Away

She threw a penny down the wishing well
Her wish was a secret she should never tell
Every day she would toss one more
Gravity made a rich girl poor

The last day came, the well she went
Last bit of change was all but spent
She waited forever and yet again
She needs some change that is heaven sent

A man then came by after a day
He was walking through the desert sand
He stopped by the well and asked her why she was crying
            All through the night
She spoke to him of empty stares, faithless men
            Greed and fear
He spoke of love so out they went
Aboard a ship of fishermen

"One penny away" they sang,
"One penny away"
Every night he would tell her that it is all right
"It is all right hey, hey, hey!"

110. Kickball

Col-de-sac games between neighbors and friends
The teams would never be even with such odd kids
We would run and slide and pitch and kick and then go home

I remember kickball after school
My small neighborhood made up such funny rules
We were never too far from our best friend's doors
I would say, "Hey there, Mrs. Holly, can Bryan play some more?"

And then came Tommy up to bat
A right foot of steel and a left arm in a cast
I swear he could kick it straight into the sun
It seems every time he is up it is a home run

Then it would get late and the next point would win
Dinner would be coming soon!
Momma's ringing their bells and the skies are a darker blue
Streetlights flickering on, and soon I am up to bat
Our team has two outs and the pitcher tilts his hat

Keep your eye on the ball
Keep it low
I swung and caught that ball whole
I swear nothing is as good as kickball
With the neighborhood

Memory #5

Sketchy behavior
Become covert
Be sly
You do not want to be seen as a goon
Jake the Waterman has come over
He has taken many forms over the years
When I do not catch a name
I am too foggy by this point in the night
Sometimes it was the day
Sometimes many days would pass
Jake the Waterman was always kind
Yet, I never got to know him
I am gone. You are gone. We are gone.
Either way I never had a good conversation.
Sometimes, I guess, the lack of conversation is all you need
These are strange memories.
Many faces with one name
Jake the Waterman

111. I will make it Work

If you would let me dry your eyes
        Wipe away your bitter mood
I want to fix the sky; the clouds have broke
        I want to bring the sunshine back to you
You have waited long enough for love
        Before this day is through
I will fix the flaw that has caused it all
        I will make it work for you
I promise you the sunrise if you put your faith in me
I promise you a lifetime if you where this shining ring

112. JAM (A funny Prophecy)

Honest music. Soulful music
Catchy music, Fun music
Dancing music, Global music
        All of this is JAM
Major chords, minor chords,
Augmented chords, diminished chords
Seventh chords, Dominant chords
        All of this is JAM
I could listen every day to music that is always changing
Miles Davis would run away if he heard any radio playing
They took what was good and turned it to ash
Good music never stood a chance
Until the gypsies rise again and kick pop music's ass

113. Evolution and God

I read a very well written book
The man had done his homework
From time elapsing and selection taking
And an eagerness for truth
Extend your hand and expand what it means to be human
Throw away theory and stare at the facts
There is no more time for believing
Mono or Poly does not interest me

Who are you? What do you want?
To be alone or to be amongst the group
If you like it join it. If you do not like it than do not join it
It is okay to not like something.
If you do not want to die than do not murder
If you do not care to die than murder!
        If you are not scared of death than congratulations
        Just attempt to care enough to not kill your neighbor

114. Dancing in the Street

Looking in the mirror
    I seem happy today
It could be because I am making lifelong friends of every race
Consistently staying up until daybreak
We will write a thousand songs with anyone who comes along

It is so exciting to worship with a new friend
It makes its mark in my memories revealing love and truth
My whole family should help me tow this line
I wish to build an empire where all souls feel alive

I cannot wait to explore newer shores
To step foot within every United State
I want to say I have seen America shore to shore
I am fortunate to be around so many cool people
We would rock and sell jam in every neighborhood

And you could carry me knowing I would do the same damn thing
We would feel so free we would begin dancing in the streets
If we are far apart I will be strong if you are weak
With a love so courageous we will be dancing in the streets
    I will sing dance with me!

115. Can I Take You Far Away?

I can bring you to a place where you never grow old
If you wish to not grow another second older
Without you in my life I would be a stone
If you let us go I will take you to my home

It is the gold and greed that destroys millions of homes
More than half alone, so half of you should know
It takes two to work things out and you are only one
I will patiently wait for you to take that jump

The place where we will go is the heart
My heart is full of love
Everything you want you can touch
Your senses will be heightened to a peak
You will be a superhero! A Queen!

And you will see you are strong
Nothing can hurt you
You and I will belong
Can I take you far away?

Sounds

Trade sounds with many minds
Walk tall with the sacred kind
Fray from thorny vines
Open your eyes in the church of lies
Follow no man into a grave
Rise up along eternal waves

116. Forty-Days with Friends

I am making my way north
I decided to take the long way
I am getting a notion
Are you teaching me?
Are you leading me closer to the answer?
        There stands a hickory door
Through the threshold lies a more colorful world

There stands a broken fence
Fix it. Give it love
        The world makes a little more sense
The wagon wheels now turn any direction
This nation is too free

I see the promise
I plan to receive what was taken from Adam and Eve
All I can see is the promise

Forty days to go
I will find my soul
I will continue down this road
I do not need directions. I want to wander
I need to wonder for now

I can see the change. I can see the shift back into my own self. I
remember this selfishness and shake my head. How could this man boy be
so arrogant? I remember trying so hard... I remember trying my best. I
remember trying to look at God through a cloudy lens and the image I got
was a distorted version of the real thing. I would relate this strongly to the
formation of religion. Religions take a concept and build absurd laws that
work for a small few (barely) and they push it towards to the masses which
stereotypically leads to violence. So sad was this young mind.

117. Laughing

Lately, I have been dreaming
        Of the day where we walk upright again
I respect every trial it took for you to knock me to my knees
        I was screaming, "Help me. Help me!"
In this limbo I am always broke and I play for fun not cash
        I feel they buy, sell and trade fool's gold preaching,
"Be the first, be never last!"

Jealousy is spawning in every direction
I do not have anything!
I cherish the happy memories
I have a future bigger than I realize
I let the past go to free me from the weight I no longer need
I feel free

I pray you will keep me up
There are no more reasons to look back to yesterday
To prove we are alone we will gather in one place
        Moments late we will be...
Laughing! Laughing so hard until we are frozen on the ground

118. <u>Leave This Station</u>

I am always expecting the worst
Too much help will cause too much confusion
This situation cannot fix itself unless there is common ground
My faceless friends will need to help

Do not let death in your way
Faking love is a quick road to him
Do not let negativity linger to long
        Be aware and weary of it
Do not end up like your mother
You will face the knife's razor edge
You will bleed out just as any human would
        Your handprints will be red forever
These men who cast the stones will end as their fathers did

If you have nothing else to say
If you have no more distractions
If you feel your beauty has been laid to rest
If you feel disgraced
        You must leave!
Purify your well!

Just hide!

From the shelter they reveal themselves
The sun may be kind
Corruption will be bound
We will force nothing!

I am leaving this station now.
I am moving to escape this Hell
I am leaving this station to purify my well
Let us get a move on!

119. Long After My Days

I see you standing so still
As clear as day he sees you wanting to be with me
That fear turns into a violent scream
So what?
                This fool cannot break you down
A woman is built to be perfect in every way
I throw my hands over you so he will never hurt you again
Do not let him have a decision on your happiness
We are lucky now to be here
Take your life back.

In our house you will ponder
How could he love someone like you?
I will love you more and more and more
To me you are perfect
I love you very much
I love you very much

Forever, you and me, face to face
I will love you long after my days
I love this place
And so you know, I love you

I saw you torn and ripped
This love took hold and sewed you
This love mended you and added to me
We as one cannot be undone

You!

120. <u>Lay Your Light Down</u>

A sudden trip takes me barefoot
I met you miles down the road
I washed your feet
You healed my heart

Lay your light upon me
Sing me a song
I was once lost in love
I now know lost love is wrong love
    But I drive across this country for you
    I will prove happiness only real when shared
I lay my light down at your feet.
A sudden trip is taking me
Maybe far out west is where I will end up
I am not sure, but I pray you think of me

And though apart you should carry on
Remember my actions and my songs
I will end up where I belong
I will cherish every soul met along the way

This light has lay down at my feet
You must sing a song for me
I was once lost in love
Once I was found it meant even more

Out of every rose I picked you
I held you close to my heart to protect you
I carried you to the top of the hill
I brought you in to my father's house
He called you a lovely flower
Worthy of royalty!

And even a prideful man would agree
You are far too good for me!
But you see me unlike them
Love has power

Wine

They always come when the wine is gone
They always call to me when their time is gone
They flourished in a field of bones
They want to walk when legs are lost
Do wrong and you will not live long!
You will work you fingers to the bone for more

121. Until the End

I told the same old story of you and the ways you would move. There is not a day that goes by where the thought of your name does not cross my mind. How long has it been? These memories seem to play around in my mind. They sometimes take the form of fantasies. Sometimes they are far from such delicacies. Until you I am alone; here with I! I wish I could paint a lovely picture of you.
I wish I could write your name within the sky to appear as diamond letters falling so fast you could not see a cloud. All that would remain in the eye would be a diamond's reflection of every hue of gold casting bullets down from the sun. His need is to brush your brow with any form of light. Love is what I need. Love from you. I want to feel something deeper than what this world can offer. And so I wait... I am getting older and that is okay. I will patiently wait for the rest of my life. How is your life? Where have you been? Did you find yourself? Do you still care about the things inside? Do you believe they see you worth as I do? As I forever will? I will love you until the end of my days. And after...

122. Run in Circles

Have you heard about these secret waters?
Have you heard about the secret land?
Could you keep a secret for me?
It will reveal everything
        Run in circles
        Run in circles
Do you know the name of every creature on earth?
Do you know the name of every star in the sky?
Could I keep one name from you?
Could I keep your own name from you?
        I run in circles
        I run in circles
So my secret...
Is it safe with you?
My deepest apologies for being so arrogant
        She loves me unconditionally
No more circles. There is too much life to live
Too much sacrifice to just give
In the name I pray for the king of kings.

123. Oh, How Far You Have Come!

I have punished myself in a twisted way
A way not okay for the king
He would scorn the thought
To hold an ounce of hatred is not okay
        To-wards me
I can honestly say I have learned from mistakes
I am cutting ties with similar ones
I making room for unfamiliar mistakes
So I can learn and grow from those too!
        Do not set in stone an interpretation
        Do not always choose the clearest path
        The meanings of these words constantly change
        A true man creates his own path
I am fumbling and stumbling around
My face hits the ground very hard
There is nowhere to go, but up from here
Rock bottom is a great place to start

Do not punish yourself during this climb!
You will slip and slide and make many mistakes
Create your own path and keep your eyes on the prize
Look back when you reach the top
And see how far you have come!

124. Santa

I heard you would be alone tonight so I tied my sack tight and left
I have many presents for you
You can choose any of them and we will have fun
Your friends have been naughty, but not you!
You are getting a spin off
Santa is coming here!

Make yourself comfortable within your home
I will come to you
I smell cookies. You grab my hat, giggle and relax
Santa is coming here!

125. We Will Rise

We continue on
You and I know right from wrong
Truth may be a poor man lives most free
Life is too short
Hold on baby, please!

Seasons changed. Did you lose yourself?
New dreams came. Did you find shelter?
Hold onto the light and pray it will not fade out
The world can change if you love a stranger more than yourself

I do not seem to mind what is happening here
You smile has filled the void
It has been killing me for years
As soon as I learned how sweet you are
I could not shake these rolling tears
A roaring lion I am for you.

I Hope You Know
Love, let me open your mind
Come with me for this ride
Do not hesitate love
Do not let no be your answer
This love is good under pressure
Let us get a little higher
Nothing gets me higher than dancing
I love stomping on the ground
I spit in the face of things that do not matter
I am forever searching and loving!

126. We Are Proud and We Love You

Feel the rain tonight
Never fear those shadows on the side
Crush the moments that leave you dry
This whole world could wither away and fade alone tonight

These moments in your imagination
I have been where you are friend
Heartbreak leaves one blind
          Welcome to a fine reality

Do you know where I was before?
I am not able to return there anymore
Lightning strikes and hits my soul
          This is my reality

This is pain I feel inside
These are emotions I try to hide
See what is wrong with me?
Can you find me lost in my reality?

Now I am outside of that shell
I can accomplish anything set in front of me
I no longer hunger for childish and foolish things
I hunger for acceptance
          Love thy mother and father

I know you love so much.
Now watch!
See what your boy can do!

127. The Dream Must Live On

I bought a pair of shoes. I gave them away
I broke a television. It led me astray
I worked fifteen hours today. I am too tired to pray
I work for glory. I am promised better days

I dream of a queen with black hair and blue eyes
I dream of a future mighty and bright
I hold fast to my loved ones
I will not see them for some time when I am gone.

I attempted to heard sheep while cloaked in sheep's skin
I have given all that a human can give
I have access to power that is not truly mine
The power of this spirit is holy and divine

I call on that strength when intentions are pure
I experience love-morphing bad into good
I have seen the demons leap from a heart screaming sin
I have even seen the good turn into evil again

There is proof to the point from the hosts we entertain
The proof is the same as it was yesterday
Time moves us forward with no time to explain
And time is no friend of eternity

Thousands of years stacked proudly
The follies of man finding new direction daily
Corporate greed and worldly dictators
A lack of patriots in a faithless world

I still pray for America and the dreams it brings
World suffering does not alleviate the desire
Forever we will live with a suffering world
Unless we allow the hopeless to be hopeful
I am calling the lost once again!

128. <u>Angel's Beating Drums</u>

It was a day like today when I realized something
There is a beauty some may never see
It is in the world. Right on it's face!
Stronger than the freedom that was given to you and me
            They asked me, "Could it be love?"
"Could it be song?"
"Could it be me if I frayed from all that is wrong?"

I laughed and said, "No! It is you and it was always you!"
"Lovely neighbors, friends and families too!"

So why are you afraid? Is it your faith?
Do you believe today is your last day?
I will bring you in and give you wine!
Together we will have the greatest loving life!

These principals may be ancient.
Some say they are from stone
My people are steadily marching to angel's beating drums

Hold on. See the world and all that it has become.
Follow me into the dark and I will show you how light overcome!

129. <u>Give Me Peace Within My Head, Lord</u>

After a while I forget I am coming up on my last cigarette
Mr. Bumblebee is swaying to the pulse of my swing
He flaps his little wings to the beat
He is watching while supporting his entire being. Floating

The wind picks up
Mr. Bumblebee is growing weak
The storm is coming
The chains on this rusted swing will break

Open up and drown out the sound of the storm
Sleep well, sleep tight, start over and let it go

Some days the world will feel heavy on your head
Gravity... everything... it all seems to keep you from achieving
I pray for you. I pray for me
Give me peace within my head
Lord, lift this weight. I pray
Give me peace within my head Lord!

130. Nothing but Perfect Times

Cheers to anybody who still believes princesses exist
Unlike vampires and sorcerers
And mermaid made for moneymaking tricks
They are living here among us
Do not you settle for a witch!
She is a diamond being hidden in a world full of greedy men

My true love came walking to-wards me down the avenue
My perspective of her on the bridge was too much to discuss
She was piercing every step
The wind made waves brushed her hair
I cherish that moment and this one too!

As hard as life is every step is for you
It is worth the struggle knowing I have you
I can see us years from now laughing how we were foolish kids
I put my hands over my face and reminisce every night

Like a dime a dozen we are always running
There is always a pretty girl on my mind
Once you are mine forever I will remember nothing but...
Perfect Times

That Smile

Lord, comfort me
I have been living merely for mortal moments
I lost my opportunity to gain a lifelong friend
I will miss that smile!

I wonder if I roam this old dirt road long enough...
Would I meet her on the other side?
If I was patient long enough...
Could she be mine?

A princess I may never see again
She is walking away towards a place I have never been
From heaven she is sent and she never leaves a trace
Her spirit I will paint as a mural in my brain
I will miss that smile!

131. Thank You for Your Time

I thank you for your time
You taught me hard work makes life all right
"IT" is life and being patient with time
The time it takes to keep composure when you are right
You know it, but their minds are riddled in pride
The lies they tell themselves keep them up at night
      Put your hands on your face and laugh
      Laugh as hard as you can for amazing grace

I cannot thank you enough
You filled my heart to the brim with love
I see you clear within everything
I sing to the skies and I sing to the great beyond
The heavens sing along
      We laugh so hard at amazing grace
      We sing and laugh at amazing grace

132. Beautiful

I am awake
No thief could take away this love
I have never been one to turn away something so beautiful

It does not show by the way you do your hair
It goes beyond the ways you move or what you wear
I will bring you closer and closer until our souls cannot tear
You are better than gold my love. You are beautiful

133. Big and Blue

Lady of war, you came into my sleep and opened my hands
My body was weak and sore; yet again I let you in
I held the purest of gold against you and watched it turn to ash
The mass of your heart did cause my ship to crash
      And as your gravity pulled me in
I saw your oceans and rivers and lakes; OH!
I saw your mountains and valleys and scapes; OH!
I will not mistake the feeling I had when I first saw you
Lovely round big and blue
      Never has a noun been as crafted as you
      A billion in the making of this great big and blue
      Never has a verb been as moving as you
      Actions speaking louder than words as you do

134. <u>Desert Home</u>

Searching for your heart
This is not a life for me if not for love
I looked in the sands of the desert
I learned from my travels man should not judge man
Imagine having the power to offer the world
Just by revealing the palms of your hands

I have seen these men who rule the world
Greed and lies worse than stealing girls
I learned from my travels I am better than no man
I would not take any riches that would steal me from your hands

I pass these legends through the world
I want to free anyone who was told,
"You are weak and weary. Let me be your man."
I am the only judge of your house upon the sand!

Desert home through you I go
I have gypsy blood and gypsy soul
I learned from my travels I should judge no man
So will you walk this earth with a stone in each hand?

135. <u>I Need You</u>

I have decided I am leaving today
I am leaving this station to purify my well
My heart has swayed my flesh
The northern town is where I will dwell

Please guide me on my way to you Lord
Give me patience and give my love strength
I have tasted your love and I want more
I need more patience, Lord, and I need more now!
    I need you all of my days
    Everyday
    I need you every single day!

Fire
Oh, brother! Do you see?
I am filled with war!
I am fluttering angrily
Brother, do you see?
There is indeed beauty in war
But, there is even more beauty within peace.
Fire is beautiful.

136. The Boy Who Cannot Sing

It is the words that come first for the boy in his mind
He hears them as hymns shaped with melody
The music then pours from his hands
Every note contains syllables and treasures for the ears

Love first, all the rest will fall like sinners to their knees
He does care, but he cannot help people who do not believe
They will never hear of the love this lame boy sings of
The silence is overwhelming to me!
I am always yearning to be taught these actions of love

True beauty is tamed by a mouth-sewn shut
It is like a magician who clips his dove's wings
Or a bastard who feels he is not enough
I hear them cheering full and proud
They are cheering for this sound coming from this boy
They thought he could not sing!

137. The EYE

I feel you watching over me
I know that you have seen all that I see
Asking father to help me for I am not alone
My demons cast out unusually long shadows
I am keeping strong to do my best
I am fighting them off to live this life with no regrets
But I am sick of needing
Could you make me whole?
Could you feed me with the time that was stolen?

Be there for me now
Hold my hand as I walk through this crowd
You shine so bright when I hold you high!
Brighter than any diamond within the starry sky

My head is feeling slow
I cannot explain this feeling I have never known
I wish I could call you out from air
To see you face-to-face to prove I am not scared
I want to show you there is more to life than meets the eye!

138. Together, Rise Above

There is one that is better than most
A crowd of many, yet one perfect host
A race was created to center around faith
They grow to fight over silly things like gold
A creature full of hate preaches of no escape
He believes a heart so pure would be a perfect trophy
For an evil man or a wolf wrapped in sheep skin

"Give into me" the serpent hisses from his tree
She was prey and gave into his convincing ways
When doubt occurred she ran into her lover and whispered
She softly said, "take!" And so he ate.

Now naked, two friends walk for hours singing and dancing
How are we lost in these woods we know?
How are we so lost in love?
That echo guided the long lost lonely traveler
For you, towards you, together we can rise above

Then it got much harder
Son, I will miss you
I cannot hold you anymore
Fray from silly things like gold

139. Forgive Me

We should have been forever
We should have been soaking up this world
            And all it has to give
I could not let you go (us two are one), so I took part in sin
Now we have knowledge from within
Love, move your lips
            Forgive I so say and then....

140. Maybe the Earth is Kind

Maybe. Just maybe the earth is kind
I do not really know
I try to open my mind, but I do not know
I know I will love you until I die
I have waited my whole life for you
A man will cry, but he will not leave you behind
So maybe the earth is kind...

Build it Up Again and Again

Lay down with me so we can talk
I am thinking as to why you are feeling gray
Are these things we can talk about today?
Do not be shy
My heart is strong enough
I will listen to anything and everything you would ask the Lord
Please close your eyes and pray
Lay down with me so we can talk
I am thinking as to why you are feeling gray
Are these things we can talk about today?
It is great you have found a home
Where would you go?
Would you just run straight into the world?
Would you risk it all on something just to watch it all unfurl?

Do not jeopardize the life you know and love and like
You will drive yourself mad with things you cannot explain
Just love your family, your neighbors and your life
Just love it all and give everything to everything
We could burn this down and just build it up again
Bigger, taller and stronger
We could burn it down and build it up again and again!

141. How Great You Are

I used to lie on my rooftop staring straight up
I would sing to the sky
I would smoke cheap cigars and talk to the pretty girl
She was lying to my right
Nowadays I lie in my bed singing songs in my head
They keep me up in the night
The world out there still remains, so I constantly wait
I am waiting for change

Hopefully one day I will laugh in the midst of a bath
With my lover at our place
I would enjoy her sweet company as I start to sing
Songs are written about her face
But for now I am locked in a cave forced to behave
Lest the future escape me
I will wait ever so patient and brave
I yearn for the moon and the stars and better days

I need to sing and dance thanking the sky
It has kept me alive to this day
It also kept me awake in the night
An infinite number of how great you are

142. In the Stars

You start a fire just to watch it burn
Rapidly rambling to the flame as she grows
Careful for you may lead my spark to your flame
And be careful because I do not chase

Her beauty will cast a shadow to lead you
She has a simple meaning to take things far
She says the answers are written in the stars

She puts it all in a lovely way
The nothing versus the every thing
Yin and yang; pursuit then blame
The admiration for a lovely game

She rolls on. She is rolling away

143. Into Space

It is lovely how your mind
It is crazy thinking that the world is ours
You carry yourself so innocent and fragile
But I know that you have a strong heart

It is lovely how you brush your long hair
It is crazy thinking about the world out there
I want to expect nothing less than magical
I know with you that is something we share

My love is far away
I have been on autopilot drifting into space
It is lovely how you walked away
It is crazy thinking what a year can change
A crippled man into a man who can walk again
It is crazy what a year can change

That distance, that lovely fire
It forever catches my eye
The light I am drifting towards
It is like a giant eye
I am moving through space
Into space

144. When Blue is Red

It is great to know that you can smile that big
A simple word turned this room upside down
       You are blue!
Just keep on laughing and I will cherish this place
These memories in my brain of an upside down room
       And you are blue

Just to stare upon a silhouette of you
Whilst laying on my mother's quilt during an odd afternoon
       Sky only blue
I will let these memories be a fantasy in my head
I will let them grow into stories passed so far down
       Blue will become red

145. Dragon Road

I have walked this far for a reason
Down an unmarked road where no soul dares to go
A voice gave me a choice to make
I chose against the voice to take a path less traveled
Filled with crooked men lusting for gold
It was Dragon Road

I know I had to go
I thought the grass was greener
With every step I take it drifts away
The notions I had of me
With every step I take I am getting closer to the link
I am looking for a story to be told

After year I would come home to show off my new shelf
But I was not recognized by a single soul
"Bandit, get back to your road!"
So call me as I am. Stamp me a liar and a thief
Disregard me as a man I will become what they speak
A monster of Dragon Road

Watch me as I go
Flying far away from home
Perfect is the place that I will reach eventually
With every step I take I am getting closer to the link
I am looking for where the sun kisses the Promised Land
There is perfect green
The fields of gold reflect the greenest of greens!

And Oh...
It is a hard life after all!

146. I Am the Box

There was a point in time where I lost vision
It was not big or small. It was just gone
The answer then came to me via dream
There was a castle
Within the walls lied the answers I would seek

I walked around and around and around
I lost my mind and began to tare all of the walls down
Thunder roared and lightning struck
I stood on the rubble of iniquity

I prayed. I clinched my fists in rage
I grabbed my hammer and split a rock
Out poured light
It sprayed out into a thousand lights of sun
A voice said, "I am the box!"

147. In This Life

I am hurting, but I am not hurt
I am lonely, but I am not alone
I am scared, but I will never stop
I am so mad because I still love you

I am broken, but I am not broke
I feel in pieces, yet you make me whole
When I am worried that I am not worthy
I hear you whisper softly, "You are my son"
So everything and all things in this life
Oh Lord, it will be for you

148. Nothing Is Irrelevant

To be in love you have to be willing to trade
The perfect day for the worst of days
It is easy to trade yourself for another
But it is hard to let it all go
For a worthy love it is worth any hurt
And to fall does not mean you will land in the dirt
For if eternity is just nothing after a life long-lived
Then I will be grateful for everything while I exist.

149. <u>We Need More Time</u>

Love, it comes in strangest forms
A realm of endless wonder all can adore
And with you love my heart is whole
My world makes sense and all I want is much more
>I have noticed in life there is plenty of falling down
>And plenty of getting back up
>Knowing the world is waiting to shove you back down
>On the ground again

Your love is enough to calm the seas
When storms within me rage and frighten families
Please make me a vessel for you lord
It is sick how the flesh can rot a man straight through his core
But I have noticed in life we constantly try to catch up
But the work is never done
We want more time for fun
We need more time to work on our faith
We need more time for love

150. Worship is an Alphabet Ahead

I hear the call of an ancient wind
This sort of natural air is long gone
It seeks revenge against an evolved calling
They want to consume me
I have grown in ways and it gives me reason to believe
Things are not as they seem
Spirits as creatures are not very sturdy beings
        Once came man, the natural world would change
He wants to better himself along with his friends
Maybe they will understand
A more complex society, a better language
Fit for comprehension
It is fit for a more intellectual conversation
He may be an alphabet ahead
        Seeping through are meaningless words
The music he plays is all to be understood
A narrow mind came wanting no man to fly
He burnt down the town and no one knew why
He searches for happiness in pain
He returns to his unhappy whore
        Then came a man to change these ways
He wanted to destroy himself
Maybe then they would understand
There was a complex plan
He knew the better language
Through praise he saw worship
He was an alphabet ahead

I, indeed, walked through a valley of death. I also swam in righteous waters. At the end of the day, I thank God for the path he put me on. I feel as if I exist in a limbo. I play for fun and not for cash. I am still playing the part. Yet, when I return to Home's Farm, I remember why I am. A legacy and a purpose are given to those who seek it. Whether living in a romance, a tragedy, a comedy, or a poetic life, there is a God who is watching. He is waiting for you to play your part. Some play the house and others play the road. I am distant enough to want the best.

I worked the land.

I left to work the world. I am eager to help my brothers and sisters. And so, I walk. I walk very far, and I work very hard.

I lift my hands and sing many songs. I write and record for those seeking. I am not perfect, but I reach everyday towards perfection.

Mentally, physical and socially I am striving and striding into a better life. I am driving towards a more perfect world. Through love you can do anything. I was bred on Southern Ground. Whether or not I understand you, I carry the knowledge of love. Love is something I cannot refuse to share with you. Within my life there has been struggle, confusion, immaturity, failure, success, laughter, sadness, madness, work, hard work, manual labors, virtual labors, yet Love leads me. I am very grateful for everything I have been handed in this life. And so, I rededicate myself every single day to reach out. I work for those who hurt. I give more water than my well should hold. When the numbers are not adding up I will continue to give because I have to. With the Lord of Lords and the King of Kings you can provide against numbers. One can conquer one thousand. With God there is rational and logic, but there is also the impossible and unexplainable.

Learn every day. Play and work. Laugh and love. Weep and mourn, so we can sing and dance. Be grateful. As this ministry began in Georgia it continues to expand in Tennessee. It is inevitable that the Bible belt will result in a world charity unlike anything mankind has seen. We are too connected to be separated... anymore. This is beauty in works. There is one Love. One Lord. North Point points north.

<u>End.</u>

PART THREE (A)...
The Staff of Moses

Opening

Up and down, back and forth
The Ladder never ends
The Lord has mercy on my soul
My future is in his hands
As I journey onward
I feel my past self-slipping by
I am eager for his Will
I stand proudly by his side

151. Half

Evil snuck into you through craft
He thought behavior was the end game
We were unable to reach her through his ways
And so we fall as pawns in sin

And so towards the purest heart they march
Forgetting themselves as light slips through dark
Memories and fantasies fade
Unless love is true

I will not be taken from you!
No gap will separate this love so true
You and I; me and you
Give me this power and I will learn to fly

So, bread keeps me from dust?
My soul will not burn lest through cold
The coldness of flesh in the ground
A body with a soul still inside!

And so I reach towards my half
She yearns too!
Two halves make a whole so we both must be saved
If I cannot make you whole... I will miss you

152. The Guard

I will be okay
I will laugh as a child today
The fall may have scraped my knees
But, now I can lead
Though we cannot play I will praise you
I will miss you.
So brave is the guard upon you bed!

153. Fire with Fire

As time elapses it is natural to question
Is there and illusion to my religion?
Is there more to this Science?
What if I just remove myself from the equation?
What if I exercise MY free will and make the problem easier?
A little less work... a little less weight... a little less hardship.
            FOR WHAT?
To miss out on this beauty.
            Think of the pendulum.
So?
            It goes left than right.
So?
            Is this not life?
No. Life also goes up and down.
There is an infinite amount of combinations directionally.
            This is not an easy concept.
Remove this direction.
            No.
Why?
            Because of the beauty
The pain
            The laughter
The tears
            Of Joy!
Of suffering
            For the betterment
Not for me
            It is not about you
If it is about humanity than explain genocide
            No
Why?
            Because that does not affect you now
So it is about me
            No
Than whom
            Do you have brothers?
Not by blood
            Do you have sisters?
Not by blood
            Do you have parents?
Not anymore
            Do you have friends?
Not anymore
            Is there nothing you can do?
No
            No job?
No

No neighbors?

No house

You do not believe that in a world full of billions of people and millions in your city that you have nothing to do and no one to help?

No

Do you believe in God?

No

Well... I do not know your purpose here. Who am I to you?

A voice in my head...

Are you not someone in need of help?

I am, but I do not want it

So it is all about you?

Yes.

That seems sad

It is.

You seem stubborn

I am.

You seem proud

I am.

You seem almighty

I am.

You think you know it all

I do.

What is the distance in centimeters from here to the moon?

I could figure it out

So you are not all knowing?

No.

So you are not God

There is no God

So what is energy?

I do not know

What are matter and or dark matter?

I do not know

So how are you so sure there is no God?

I do not know. I do not care. I am agnostic

What does that even mean?

It means I do not care

Than who am I?

A voice in my head

Why?

I do not know, but I wish you would shut-up!

Why?

Because I am sick of questions with no answers...

Like the half assed answers, you give me?

Yes.

Than answer me one question...

Okay...

Why do you not care?

Because I am scared...

God can fix that.

Again with this nonsense!

154. More Questions

Am I capable of becoming someone more logical?
These theories have created a nice escape
But if there was a creator, why is there not world peace?
And if there is no creator... why am I here?

155. The Power of God

I think the peace you seek is not the peace promised
Is there not peace in our galaxy?
Is the earth not tilted just so for you mortals?
Are the oceans not subsided just enough?
Is the land not plentiful enough?
Are the fruits not sweet enough and plants not green enough?
Are the people not vast enough for your picky taste?
Are your idols not shiny enough?
Wine not thick enough?
You want and want and want so much it surpasses your needs.
Who are you to me?
Small! Yet I love you so much
You step on an ant and do not think twice about it.
I could crush your universe the same way.
But I love you

One slight tear in your gravity and you would be catapulted into extinction. I could destroy a planet fifty times bigger than the sun and send its mass directly towards you. I could turn all of the lights out and watch you suffer in the dark. I could destroy you fast or slow. I could keep you alive for myself just to watch you suffer. I could send you to an eternal prison. These are my powers. Yet, I love you. I want you. You sin and hate and do these things to one another. Yet, I love you still. You selfish, egotistical, beautiful creation... I love you... please love me. I will give you immortality if you love me. Everything you desire if you are patient and wait. Just love me forever, and I will continue to do the same.

Months

I have missed many months
I made a life changing decision for the Lord
Oh, these decisions!

I do not know right from wrong
I am not the judge to the stranger
I only judge my brothers because I know them

I do not refuse love anymore
I refuse these conditions
For her sake and mine

I must be challenged
I have a lot of work to do
I will give you nothing less than my best
Your Will is my Will
Forever and always my love

156. Hierarchy

Why did man create hierarchy?
Is it the necessity to follow and worship?
From priests to prophets
From Shamans to Kings
From Political Science to the Science of Religion
How non-religious people get to fly...

It is a comical randomness
These things are determined through nonsense
Yet, they all have purpose
Are you determined to destroy theories with theories?
Are you a hypocrite fighting fire with fire?
You have a lonely existence you who fight fire with fire
        Try to fight fire in your personal hell.
        Good luck my bold friend.

157. A Life Changing Thought

I keep this moment frozen in time
I hold it near to my heart and my word
To contrast, I am on fire for you
This fire does not consume
       You say yes
You are now mine
This beautiful contrast keeps my eye
The love of this moment frozen in time
My love, in one day, will drift far away
I will resurface amongst the dust
I will return as this clay
Today, I reflect on a life changing thought
Will I choose to leave my friends?
Will I remain close to foes?
Which is which? Are you friend or foe?
Should I just go?
Lord! Please teach me right from wrong!

158. Reach the Moon

I will be home when I reach the moon
I am lucky; I am crazy; I am a loon
I will paint a picture for you
With words, describe the light of the night

Can you feel the pull of the Hunter's Moon?
Is your heart light? Are you doing all right?
A rapid man from the man on the screen
He tells me of a man that holds infinite love

A thought becomes aroused.
I want to return
He will purify my blood
Where it all started

I will be home when I reach the moon
I am lucky; I am crazy; I am a loon

159. <u>Trip</u>

I could sleep in
I could take a walk on the beach sand
I could carry you within my hands
       Or we could lye for a while
Take it all in, the soft wind
Breeze rolling on our skin
Late I will sing to you on the pier
We will watch the sun set behind the small trees
       In the distance
Simmer down at dawn
Cool off in the spring
Thirty years go by
We will smile at the memories

160. <u>Life's Finer Things</u>

Within those eyes lies a precious thing
The picture of a treasure and I can only see a piece
It is in that lovely look and gaze
The beauty has found its place

I cannot find them yet
The words and the courage
I need to cast away this shell
I do not need who I used to be
I have built a fire
From these ashes will raise the best of me

Lord
       I pray for the promises that you bring
       A dream of life's finer things
Lord. Oh
       I praise the fire that crafted me
       And for my dreams
Lord
       I pray for the peace I find in you
       In peace I can believe
Lord. Oh.
       I pray for you to take my heart, so take it gently
       On these ashes stands a man, he has had all he can take

This Song
I still give my all
I will give it all until all I have is gone
I give you all until all that remains is faith and hope and love
These memories made within these moments
And so we write this song

161. The Beginning of this Language

I wish to create a new language
Or maybe I should redeem this old language
I can only use senses available to me

My eyes witness love
            Reveal my soul
My ears hear your voice
            Reveal my soul
My nose breathes in life
            Reveal my soul
My mouth sings you praise
            Reveal my soul

My hands play for you
My music is for you
I know you
I hear you
You listen and give me sound!
Your vibrations are soft and powerful!
Reveal the beginning of this language

162. Oh Savior

It was supposed to be me
All by myself
Walking over to the turnip truck
But, you were right beside me
Coming in my head
Coming in my heart
Just to say, "hello"

I courted you while wandering
"Why choose me to play this part?"
I love playing along to this music
Just loving every second
Keeping all of the lights turned on
            Oh Savior! I am in need of saving
            Oh praise, oh praise, oh praise

163. Release and Peace

Lord, release to me a vision of peace
Give me a piece of you
Your soul within my soul
I need something to direct my worship towards

How I cherish the one of forty-two seconds
            That second when I am with her
That one sixth of a day times seven
            How I cherish every moment when I show her!
Though I can only show her as much as she will allow
            We have not even scratched the surface!
Love, I can give you the greatest loving life
            I can give you the greatest life!
This peace I seek may be the love of another...
            She may be too wonderful to believe
Too precise for man to conceive

I have been having vicious dreams of who I used to be
I have been waking in the night asking for your hand to lay on me
I have been tossing and turning; sweating and thinking
I have been holding irrelevance too close to my heart

I wish I could let go
It would be easy to forget
I am glad these trials make me unique
Yet, do not let them steal your glory!
My rope has been twisted one too many times
Too many knots causing this ladder to be rendered useless
Knots may allow one to climb up a rope...
Yet, it shortens the distance of the rope
Is safety worth shortening the rope entire length?
Is this sacrifice?

This could assure the saving of one life versus many
Maybe it is the strong that survive.
Strength of a different source
The meek, the weak, the humble, the merciful
The ones who can follow

I feel I was given leadership when I should have followed
Maybe these are my demons...
Either way, I pray for release. Release and Peace

164. The Greatest Love Story

Oh, how many great talks occur in warm waters
From oral stories and from personal experience
I am limited in knowledge
I am infinite in love

I try to speak for something believed to be above
I need to pitch a perfect line
One that can pass through the sands of time
Robbers and thieves alike
They grind their teeth and roll the dice
They will never find love within anything money can buy
The true love in need of purchasing is love
What can drive all of us forward is... love
What could end all world hunger is... love
What could separate man truly from the world is...
What could bring the father back is...

Could is hopeless. Can is profitable.
The Greatest Love Story can exist.
And so it does

165. Driven

I have already driven the miles to know I am small
I have seen the earth from afar; I know I am small
I have been suspended in space and I know I am small
I have already thought the hours to realize I am alone
I have been with you and I have left you
I may be alone in my head, but my heart is full for you
Because of you, I am not alone in my heart
I am so happy to be aware of the great love story
It begins and ends very day with you!
This is more than a drive. It is the Will

Ready for Change
She is ready to love
Ready the horses
She is ready to change
Follow the Course
She is ready to love
Man up and hold her
She is ready to love today!

166. Catching Up

I love catching up with her to see what has not changed
I am drawing her back in with newer songs on newer days
She points at the King and the Queen to reveal something new
There is a change in her eyes sparkling white against sky blue

167. A Love Letter

I have discovered a universe within my own mind
A God-Like ability to come and go as I please
I am curious as to why my brother is lost within his
He is the God of his own mind; he should be able to leave it

Maybe the reason as to why is because he is stuck!
Is this some form of pride or a form of free will?
Does free will not exist in his Universe?
I am not he; so I cannot save him... Who can?
Is it truly choice if you do not know you are lost?

I fear that my brother does not know that he is lost
But then again, I am lost!
I do recognize that my abilities were formed through my accord
Yet, I recognize that something helped me
Seventeen thousand years...
          Could not save a man who wants to be...
Lost within his own self

Although I may come and I may go,
I will always return to you at the end of the day
I will say thank you for everything you have given me!
This is not by choice.
I am cursed to love you forever

A love letter to my sinful nature
Until deaths do us part.

168. Lay the Weapons Down

A right to bear arms
Lay your weapons down.
Mental restrictions are just as dangerous as physical ones
Is it not insane building a seven-lane highway and it still become
jammed as if no construction or expansion was done?
Rushing through life with anxieties unnecessary
We have zero worries
Are you not trapped in traffic whilst going on vacation?
Going on vacation to happily lose your mind

Our love so special; driving me like this car every day
I would not trade it for anything my girl
Infinity means nothing since I have met you
Do not trade that for anything love
Remember this love when I lay you down
Remember this love and lay your weapons down
Remember me when you lay down
Lay all of your weapons down!

169. <u>Yes, I Can!</u>

I am wishing I could slow this train
I have been wandering for so long
If God could stretch a right hand down
I would be grateful for the thought
        No one seems to care
        People seem content being alone
        In a selfish way I am too
        It is a poor excuse for hope
Oh Lord, here my cries
I am longing for your soul
I am longing to be taken home
I am sick of being alone
        Sometimes, I feel my prayers fall on deaf ears
        Sometimes, I feel there is no way out
        I must be patient because one day I will know
        I will be with you again
Lord, please let me see your face
I know it would separate me from this human race
Maybe I could stand a chance
I want to be worthy of your grace
        If Jesus and I walked side by side
        Could you point out the difference?
        Would we be so similar or unalike?
        Would you question if we were kin?
I know I am not living right
I know I have weak and shaking knees
I know these are troubling times
And I know you forever love me

170. Boys at Battery Lane

So the boys and I were gathered at the old rope swing
The layout of this stream is a curious thing
If you feel too short you would bust your ankles on the rocks
The middle was the sweet spot because too far, you'd take off

One day I was high on life, so I grabbed the old rope swing
I took off looking like a fool to get that girl to look at me
I took it too far and the rapids stole my knees
I was shooting for the sweet spot, and I found myself downstream

I could not breathe; I could not see a thing
I wound up on a stranger's shore laughing hysterically
Her shadow peeked over me asking if I was all right
I slicked my hair back and said, "Better since you arrived."

One day I was high on life, so I grabbed my dignity
I took a chance looking like a fool to get that girl to laugh at me
I took it too far, though she smiled; she slapped my cheek
I was shooting for the sweet spot and I found myself downstream

Well she was the prettiest thing my tired eyes had seen
The missing piece of the puzzle; the girl of my dreams
Not a second to waste because she had me on my knees
The current took me far and now she has me

One day I was high on life and I saw beauty in everything
God has placed her in my life to get this fool to start caring
When I take it too far you just have to smile and kiss my cheeks
I will be shooting for the sweet spot ending up way downstream
                Downstream in love

The Language of the Angels
Music to me is more than just sound
It is the vibrating language of the angels and freedom if you're bound
Let everything that is light from within shine outward
When you are tempted by the demons do not give in

Lord, open up my mind and let me see your face
I have been alone before and I am sacred there are darker days
But the Lord of light will make everything okay
Lord, with you, my life has been more than okay

Love alone to me is an all-consuming fire
It does not destroy!
Amazing in the least
Happiness it brings
How can something be so perfect to me?
How can perfection respect me?
I am a sinner in the morning
I am a loser and I am weak

Let the language of the angels tend my bitter heart
Let them repair my brittle faith
Let these questions be answered
Love always conquers hate!

Learn to speak the language of the angels
Listen to sweet love's amazing grace

171. Horizon's Song

You are so beautiful
That is exactly what you are
Hop into my boat
We can take this far away from here
You voice is magic to my ears
Everything you say seems to make this life more clear
Away! We should go!
We can teach the world what we know. We can show the world

I can still see you at certain points in space
Burned in my memory
This love will not fade
This love will never fade away
I have existed within a perfect day
It was you and I
Swinging through a Sunday
A hammock in the shade
A mist of creek and rain

My mind will never be the same
Your love is color to my brain!
Lovely lady, you must stay
Lovely lady, you must stay
Your beauty alone will drive me insane

This life takes us towards horizon's love
Let gold sky meet dark blue as horizon's song
We will dance all the night until the moon goes away
We will all lose our heads

Lord, I am too anxious in far too many ways
Mostly for the future and the history we will make
Just know I am your anchor and I will be a great escape
I will walk you towards the Pearly Gate
I will never change
The Alpha and the Omega will never change

172. <u>Over A Girl</u>

Hey my love, you look lovely today
If I may, I would like to take the time to tell you a tale
It is about a boy who has fallen in love
And this little boy is becoming a man

She sings songs within her head of stories similar
Yes, her soul has longed and dreamed of this day
And she just smiles and turns away
She says, "I am not ready. I am a small, little, foolish girl"

She is making you wait to test you
She wants to see how far you will go
How far will you go?
She loves to watch you twist and struggle
It is funny how we lose our minds over a girl
Little foolish girl!
Small, little, foolish girl

I am waiting to fly across the ocean
To settle in a town awaiting something new
Wait for me love! I am coming!
I am excited to settle in a homeland
To start a new life and create new family friends

173. <u>1567</u>

After a virtual Sunday morning service
I was eager to meditate
I needed to get out of the house
I needed nature's sweet escape
Strangers overpopulated my secret spot
They were in search for the same
I ventured out from the watering hole
I walked towards a mountain two miles away

An empty lot caught my eye
I hiked up a very steep hill
So unique... tucked away gently
It had enough terrain to satisfy

I continued around the bend
This spot left me in AWE
The greatest property overlooking Nashville
1567

A vision and a dream released to me
This valley is mine for the taking!
My heart began yearning
My mind began churning
I will get that spot
First, every dream must be unlocked

174. A Light for You

I have never noticed this type of sky
And now I always wander why
Why do people not look up more often?
I attempt to explain this within my mind

I just do not trust in my own answers
I just do not trust a feeble and stirring mind
I do trust in you!
I trust in your guidance to guide me through
I want to be a light for you

And so you guide me through these dark streets
I wander where we will meet?
I wander what you will show me
How will I end up where I am supposed to be?
I can travel safe and far because your light is on me

Because of this light, I am aware
I am aware of what is ahead as far as the eye can see
I can prepare to make the turns approaching me
I am preparing for the distance
When my turn comes, I will choose

I have realized the path does not matter
Whether a bright path or a pitch black path
As long as I shine my light for you
I do not even need a lamp
I can be light for you
I can be a light for you

175. I would give it Up for You

I have run dozens of miles with a heartache
Running far from you
I have since searched for love in strange places
I wanted to avoid making memories of you

I may not know if this world is fine
There are too many creatures lurking in the dark
The shadows make a safe place to live
If you are hiding from love

Understand that I know you!
I would lay down my pride for you

The night my eyes first lay on you is written in poetry
A holy kiss within ten thousand faces happened to be you and me
I finally felt my broken road had a beautiful meaning
God's hand had been walking me through darkness
He was guiding me towards you.
He was making me strong for you!

I may not know if this world is fine
But I would give it all for you
My one true love
I would give it all

Let Me Fall into Love

My favorite dreams are when we hold hands
Though I am fast asleep, in those dreams you sink me in
I am falling too deep in this dream
And in this love you are casting on me

Let me fall into love with you
And let you fall into love with me

I have live life casted out into dirt
I have walked through the darkness
I have experienced the worst
But, I listen to the Lord
He says to me,
"There is no need to be afraid"

The light of this love shines brighter than the sun
There is a world with no shadow
Let me take you to this world
Listen when I say,
"My God and your God...
Made us to not be afraid!"

LOVE:
Let me fall into love with you
And let you fall into love with me

176. Dance with Me

There is one phrase that repeats in my head
I would be a fool to let you go
I am running to the ends of the earth
I am singing, "No diamond shares her worth."
Understand that no diamond shares your worth love.

Would you let me be you armor from this world?
Would you let me be your transportation?
Would you let me be a rock where you can stand?
Would you let me kiss your lips and hold your hand?
As we dance
Dance with me
All I am saying is I will be patient
For you my love!

177. Oh Light!

A cave man's eyes will never see outside
This is because he lives in a cave
He misses every sunrise and the magic of the light
As sunrays fall upon and then lift off of this city

And most men at desks never feel the sun
They are too content with sitting still
They miss all of the warmth and the magic of the light
Let sunrays blanket and then retreat from this sad city

Every moment between dawn and dusk hold infinite space
It holds infinite love
The beauty between you and me is beautiful
Oh Light, Oh!

I met a ninety-three-year-old lady some days ago
She had a strange request within our conversation
She asked me for some ice cream
She asked me to go outside
She said, "Lift your nose up to the sun."
She said, "Feel this light!"

Oh light, oh.

Today I am reminiscing and simply craving the sweet life. This is the life that I know is out there. I have tasted it as I have tasted the sweet honey produced on Home's Farm. I am thinking about the moment when I knew I would be returning. I am dreaming for the day when I return to my Home that lays within the Green Hill of Nashville.

I miss the music. I miss the friendship. I miss the hard work and the dedication to the Project. Poetry seems to be the constant within my life. Poetry seems to be the thing that has always been there for me. Even as I continue my education I daydream about the day when I return. I will return. I do not know how, and I do not know when, but I will return.

178. <u>Ishtar</u>

I came to Ishtar wearing only sackcloth
She was a beautiful beast on a purple couch
We rolled for hours and only spoke two words
I said you and she said I

Every leg left the floor
They pointed towards the starry sky
Every hand hard at work
My tongue bounds by hers
        Now every servant is serving
        Some begin dying
        No one can satisfy this woman!
        Ishtar!
You took me in as a stranger in this town
She pulled me deep into her breasts and she knew I was hers
Another slave to serve her majesty
She took my honor and placed it in a jar
After I buried it as deep as deep can go
Into this earth I will drown in dirt
She kept begging for more

Ishtar! You spoiled bitch
You want it all and I want you to have it
I gave you all I had and you took it proudly
AND THEN YOU WATCHED ME DIE

I marvel at the fact all men know what I do know
Yet, I will not let go.
Ishtar!
We know you know we know!
Ishtar!

    This woman steals my breath away in the worst of ways. She stares me down with no remorse of what she is about to do to me. I am eager to see when she makes her first move towards my soul. Should we stay late and get to know one another a little better? I think I should keep my distance. This woman may be the one who finally steals me away. She stares at me in the worst of ways. She is pushing her Cougar Love.

179. Dawn of the Day!

There have been ups and there have been downs
Closed doors and open doors
My version of life and then yours
There have been boxes and many doors

Tonight I will dream
I am; I am
I am the sky
I am the dark of the night
I am the light of the day

Sweet summer sweat
Cold winter burns
The innocence of spring
The wisdom within autumn
  The beauty in this twisted world
  The beauty within everything
  The art within nothing
  The art this love may bring
I am patiently waiting
I am waiting to touch this love
We are slowly gathering
Due to this touch
  And as we wait we will dream!
I am. I am the sky. I am the dark of the night
I am the dawn of the day!
  And as we wait we will dream
I am. She is the sky. He is the dusk of the night.
We are the dawn of the day!

180. The Wedding Tree

Sitting under the Wedding Tree
Thinking of her knowing she's thinking of me
Smoking strips amongst a band of banjos
Smoking cigarettes amongst a band of thieves

A band of thieves are coming
To rummage this old town on horses
They are driving towards a sunset behind darkened clouds
On white, black, and red horses

A fortnight will fly by as quickly as a blinking eye
You will wait an eternity longing for her familiar smile
And as patient as you are there is a far more patient God
Longing for your odd shaped heart to return to the stars
Like a trophy in a jar

The Ladder to Paradise

When I attempt to recall prior days...
My mind creates walls I cannot get through
Nor can I escape the entrapment
I am just trying to recreate
I want to share one experience during this break

It seems every other hour is filled with nuances and clatter
So this silence is the best time for me to write
Forms of fiction here and there
This may be art, but I will not write about her
Words cannot describe what I feel inside

It is time to be me
Consumed in a strange love
It is also time to experience everything
I am ready for the world
The world in arms for the Lord
I am sharing this with my love
I hope she understands
She needs to be in his arms
The Lord will guide her to him

Together we will climb the ladder of Jacob

181. Dear Friend

My hands are tied my dearest friend
I part from you now to join this here woman
I am out on my knees asking her in
I would cut out my heart for her dear friend

My legs have been bound my dearest friend
I have given my will to live with this here woman
I have sold my lot to bring her in
My inheritance gone for her dear friend

She shows me fire and teaches right from wrong
I will live the rest of this life
As if it is song

I am strapped to this chair my dear friend
She is cutting my hair and I am breathing her in
I am bearing much fruit, as much as one can
I am living in love, but I miss you dear friend

You taught me honor, loyalty, and song
You taught me how to love and how to pass it along

Though bound I feel free amidst this land
I am lost in these moments breathing her in
He skin is as soft as feather brushing my hand
Always living in love, but missing you dear friend

You taught me honor, loyalty, and song
You taught me how to love and how to pass it along
She shows me fire and teaches right from wrong
I will live this life out as if it is song

182. <u>Slow Summer Days</u>

Slow summer days and inside I remain
I get out when I can, but under roof I must stay
I wait patiently while they travel and play
I am working for a future unknown

Slow summer days, first half dry and second half rain
My lady is out so my soul is on break
I wait and wait to serve her one more day
My heart feels wrenched when my love is away

Slow summer days drifting away
As I grow older my child mind remains
Slow summer days where the predators prey
I work and I work so my lady will stay

Boisterous sounds
There are two parts to this book of Moses
To build on the poet with more poetry!
I try to arrange and imitate these sounds from the head
The sound is unique, and the message is also boisterous

183. <u>Ink</u>

I can smell the ink
It lingers heavy in the air
From scribble on paper
Into directing insanity

I think of selfish desire
Come out tonight
I will not pout
If she is alright

Keep me strong and brave
Let me learn and love the same

184. Matthew 7:28

I am hurting Lord.
My heart cannot take this pain
Through my heart is a broad sword
I am afraid I will never be the same

How can this be? What have I done?
To deserve this pain and load
Is it because I love MY God?
Is it because I once was bitter and cold?

Is Karma the reason my reach falls short
Do I not deserve good love?
I would have wed her in the court
If you let it be from above

I know YOUR will means not my own
Let these selfish desires float away
I will chase you now, forevermore
Until the end of my hearty days

185. Genesis

In the beginning was the Eye
Extending into eternity
The Eye took in light
Simultaneously becoming light
       Over time spawned the heavens and earth
       Water subsides and up comes dirt
       Life would come next, though I do not know how
       I was not there, but I am here right now

Meter
I read a poem
I read a poem
Eye red a poem
A red apron
A rad acorn
A unicorn
I owe you a nickel
I do not have a nickel
Do you have a nickel?
Can I have a nickel?
I do not need a nickel
There is no meter near here
Or is there?

186. Listen

Reading is good when you read out loud
It is a beauty alone how the words all fall out
I need to listen better
        I am not a good listener
        I pray I become a better listener
I need to learn more
        I am not a good learner
        I pray I become a better learner
I need to love better
        I am not a good lover
        I pray I become a better lover

187. So Much Anger

So much anger
I also have lapses
My mind is foggy and I lose sight of life
I lose sight of the important things
I want to be love
Something this world may not be fond of
Love and worship
Until the end of my days
Love and worship

188. Evangelize 1st and Broadway

Strange mercy shown through callused eyes
Once again I am up against pride
As long as your heart beats there is hope for you
Let the Eye reveal how one should cut dangerous ties

With the light shining you become radiant
You cannot help but reach towards her corroded feet
Dangerous ideas spill from their gutter
They pollute this river with evil
And so they may get baptized in sin
Unless the light is pure white

I cannot save this woman
I simply leave it up to the Lord
Take care of your daughter
She is tormented by legion

189. Yellow Balloon (revisited)

I love when life gives me an interesting day
Whether a coincidence or something you can't explain
At the end of each day I thank God I have you
As sweet as candy and candles and yellow balloons

You lift me up when I am feeling blue
Just being you lightens up my mood
That one word from you puts a smile on my face
Like a yellow balloon on a dark grey day

Hitchhiking through Georgia on a red dirt road
I needed one last lift so I could get back home
It was very unlikely cars would come down this way
I fell to my knees and I started to pray

Lord, I need luck! I don't know what to do
Just like that, the man upstairs pulled through
A long lost friend with a grin on his face
Driving a big yellow bus on this dark grey day

He said, "Hey friend, aren't you looking good
Hop on in and tell your boy where to"
I said, "Take me on home, my love has been worried sick
My supper is cold; she's looking for her switch"

We cracked up! We talked about the good news
A little honor and luck can turn a grey sky blue
The sun started shining on this house of grace
My love ran on out planting a kiss on my face

Love lift us up towards the sky so blue
A little honor and luck if you know what to do
One simple word can put a smile on my face
Like a yellow balloon on a dark grey day
It is love

190. The Director and the Dictator

The director and the dictator were walking side by side
Twas a beautiful autumn day and the town was much alive
The dictator saw a family being married under his tree
The director glanced and both began to walk towards the scene
The dictator began to speak a most negligent way
He hated the thought of happiness apart from him within this day
It reminded him of his last wife he left ten years ago
The director new about this tale and also never let go
His sister was the bride and the other was a friend
He could not accept this happiness existing beyond his hand
The dictator easily would condemn all against his will
The director did not mind and so she simply sat still
The dictator ordered every soul to be hung on the tree
The director simply nodded and led the whole conspiracy
Not every tale will end with happy-go-lucky song
When dictators lose heart the directors also retire

This Time is Different
I feel as if I am drowning
I need to be woken up
Playing music has a purpose
I should get out and set-up
I am stuck in a loop of work
Bi-weekly checks and all
I love my life in Nashville
But comfort is not what God wants
I want to work hard and become this love
I want to be a leader and give many people jobs
Give me strength as I go down this road
This time it is very different

191. Two More Years

Another two years
Look at all that has become of me
I am not who I used to be
Just give it another two years
In two more years I will once again be different
In two more years I will have newer friends
In two more years I will be happier
In two more years it could be my end

192. Honey Chugging Bear

Honey chugging bear
        Cooking up a meal
Fish and rice again
        Ten for ten a deal
He cooks all day for his friends and his Texas family

Sonatas about birds
        Whistle me a humble tune
Harmonize that cello into thirds
        Major or minor will either do
He plays all day, but not for his family

Strange is a bear that cooks and plays with cello
Strange is a cat that hasn't met her fellow

Kitty has been caught within a net
        And eaten by a wolf
Wolf eaten by the bear
        Chased down with honey until full
And then become what every man fears most

Part bear, part wolf, part cat... and mostly honey
Half bear, half wolf, half cat... and mostly honey

Demonstrate to me pretty lady if you can
How can three halves make a hole and still have room for honey?

Strange is a bear that cooks and plays with cello
Strange is a cat that hasn't met her fellow

193. <u>The Tree that Owns Itself</u>

I am the tree that owns itself
Grace has given me a place
Amongst this earth and rubble
Lives a legend; lives a faith

A song is written to represent
My beauty, I am the Oak
My pure and fervent energy
Bellows stories thick as smoke

When Father stood upon this ground
He was aware of his own faith
Now I, the son, reside on this mound
I own all around my base

Centuries lives this legend
Centuries more it will go on
I am the tree that owns itself
I stand for freedom, love, and eternal song

194. <u>Without You</u>

I am calling out to you to save me
Save me from myself
I give you all I am; I give you everything
New friends, old friends, lurk within
Athens
This dirty place becomes
Home away from homes
My heart is tight; I feel insane
It makes me feel alive
Or am I already dead?

Strangely though I feel alive
Chase the chance to witness and shine
Scorn the awkwardness
Applaud the honest

Nothing matters without you
I do not care about money if I cannot spend it on you
I do not care about music if I cannot play it for you
I do not care about this life if I cannot live it with you

195. You and I

You and I walking side by side
You and I
Midst a garden, the serpent still
Yet, you and I
I held you in, called you by name
It's you and I
I bring you in for I still love you
And you and I

Oh! How fast the middle of the day passes by
When You and I

I think of war, I lean on you
The Lord, the Eye
I dream of her, I dream of you

Oh! How fast the middle of the day passes by
Every time I see you
Reveal the Eye

You and I walking side by side
Just you and I

Like the Tree

Circle around my many friends
Walk these broken roads hand in hand
Take and own this hell
As a tree that owns itself
Its many roots spread far and wide
A vast grapevine producing the sweetest wine
Take and own this hell
As a tree that owns itself

You have held out for so long
But only by a single thread
You must take and own this hell
As the tree that owns itself
I tell you now the time is near
Raise your hands and hold your tears
You must take and own this hell
As the tree that owns itself

Lift up your cup and drink your fill
Break free from chains; retrieve free will
You must break the chains themselves
You must own life as a tree that owns itself

196. I Will Sleep Tonight

Tonight I will not sleep
I might be late another day
I am sorry if I am
I haven't slept well in many days
I just do not think I can
Plans have all changed and I do not mind
If I can get a job
I want to save some dollar bills
I do not want to just give up
If I go back to where I came from I will feel I'm at a loss
Riches may reside there, but for my soul... at what cost?
Athens is a fantasy if all went our own way
But I know man's intent and free will never fare does play
People are the most complex of nature's creations
And humble is a mind that lives to serve his fellow man
I am still in search of the most loyal of sons
I wonder how I could meet him
I am still in refusal to praying
But I am willing for a lesson
I will serve for the remainder of days
This will be my story
A servant for my fellow man and a soldier for God's army
I will not spill a drop of blood for there is none within my cup
I must say I am embarrassed for I have already drank mine up
I couldn't wait to taste it because impetuous is my game
It is in my genes to go all in and in my breath to do the same
I want to practice what I preach so I can walk on coward's back
I will use them as my stepping stools to reach the highest path.
And so, I sleep for now.

197. I See You On the Hill

Oh, I see you; Oh, I see you
Oh I see you on the hill
I have been there; I have been there
I have been there standing still
       Though my heart sings to you song
       And I am right where I belong
Worshipping all the day long
Oh, I see you on the hill

Lord, I thank you; Lord, I thank you
Lord, I thank you for your will
I was lost Lord; I was lost Lord
I was lost and now I am filled
       And my heart sings to your song
       And I am right where I belong
Worshipping all of the day long
Lord, I thank you for your will

Oh, I see you; Lord, I see you
Lord, I feel you here with me
I was lost Lord; I was tossed Lord
I was kicked and left to bleed
       And now my heart sings to your song
       And I am right where I belong
I stand before my Lord in song
Oh, I see you on the hill

198. I Worship Today

I come to you oh God; I worship today
I come to you oh God; I worship today
You save me! You saved me today!
       I pray to you oh God; I worship today
       I pray to you oh God; I worship today
       You save me! You saved me today!
Oh God, in Jesus name, I worship today
Oh God, in Jesus name, I worship today
Lord save me! Save me today!
       Lord, mighty to save, I worship today
       Lord, mighty to save, I worship today
       You changed me; you changed me today
Holy is the name I worship today
Holy is the name I worship today
You saved me; you overcame the grave

199. The Man at the Commodore

> I have listened to a dozen men sing a dozen sad songs
> They all shared one thing... a lost love when they were young
> And I have heard of heartbreaks since I was a boy
> But to be a man and live it has its own sick reward
>
> There are two empty seats at the table where we'd eat
> There is a lonely bed, always made, where we used to sleep
> At my lowest of lows, I seemed to find a place
> Now I lie in the hands of God with a yearning for his grace
>
> So everything and all things in this life
> Lord, it will be for you
>
> A poor man sang a song about a friend who did him wrong
> He did it in the name of God and said, "Boy, you should move on!"
> Cheers to the twenty-seven years recovering from the hurt
> Now that man is writing songs, and he is reading the good word
>
> He said, "OH! Everything and all things in this life
> Lord, it should be FOR you!"

200. The Poet's Dream

She stole my heart as soon as she walked through those doors
I knew I was signing off from that solo life
I swore I would never be a man who settled down so easily
> I saw myself living the poet's dream
> Forever love, just you and me
I trotted on thin ice and then I wound up at the pub
They played me "Galway Girl" I saw myself in love
This should not be
Good luck was never too fond of me
> I found myself living the poet's dream
> Forever, Lord, You, her and me

I've yet to figure out how all this life is lived
If not for love I would best demonstrate
How easy it can be to fill the heart so full of hate
There's space so empty when love's gone or just misplaced
I trace this back to you; true love is not erasable
> We dance

A New War

A new war is being fought
Spiritual warfare in the heavens
It ripples out into earth
it steals the youth away in vengeance

An example stands in black lives
All of their lives matter
They war with one another
Especially with big brother
They war within the streets
Forgetting freedom and peace
Remember Dan Bullock
He fought for freedom

I want to honor this man on my mind
Far more than Brown or Black in '69
I believe fifteen is too young
Yet he gave his life for mine
He gave his life for our rights
Near most fifty years ago
This boy got on a plane
To be the youngest soldier
In the bloody Vietnam Games

Black lives matter
BUT... just the same as white
Just the same as brown, yellow, red
Just the same as mine
So why do we fight?
I believe the cross is a plus sign
Come together in love
A new war is being fought

201. Patiently Waiting

I am patiently waiting to be busy again
I am nervous and anxious in far too many ways
I am looking forward to making new friends
I will dance knowing I am in a good place

I am here to seize opportunity
I am looking for doors and making the most
I need to pray and save and develop immunity
Then I can go back into the world as a healthier host

202. <u>Goodbye for Now...</u>

Tonight I pick up my cross
I start walking to-wards Calvary
I feel I am at some loss
Yet, I refuse to become charity

I can carry my own weight
As long as the Lord provides me strength
I am listening and pushing for you
I am wishing to be guided towards truth

Love me little; love me long
Love me right and love me wrong
Love me if I aim to kill
Forever and always, love me still.

Goodbye for now my dearest friend
I forever long to see you again
I know now I must let you go
Let the Lord carry away this sorrow

Goodbye for now my one true love
I am sorry my love was not enough
I am burdened to see you go
But I must walk this Holy Road

Goodbye for now my heart and home
Goodbye to those hills I used to roam
With my companions by my side
Goodbye my love, Goodbye my pride

Goodbye forever my useless self
I sentence your spirit straight to hell
You have cast your last jagged/wicked stone
Goodbye my demons, God saved my soul!

203. Workshop Visions

Could I be you?
Or are you me?
If we are us I may be she

If I am he and they are we
Are you the one who calls for me?
Or is she the you who say we are three

I am not three for I am one
Unless you and I than I am us
And if we are together while you are there
We all exist so who should care.

I meet many new people
They are all so unique
Yet, I feel I have met them before
Time and space are getting weak

The closer I get the more power I have
And this power is a dangerous thing
I pray for guidance along this new path
I pray I remain humble and meek

I pray for the day when I can love unashamed
And us two will be forever one
I pray I can wait for that glorious day!
When the bride and the groom merge under the sun

So, come my sweet and I will take you in
I will take you in with all of your ways
I broke within and lost many friends
And now I am forever changed
By grace and love and hope and faith

204. New Guy

Being the new guy is hard
Especially when you are not the new guy
The other guy is the new guy
So I must make a friend
Unless I do not want to
Than he is out of luck
But my father would be disappointed
If I did not give him a shot
                    So, "Hello new guy!"

205. <u>More to Love</u>

Love, you are not wasting time
I have been there before
You think there is something else
When love is at your door

Yes, more can meet the eye
When you exist to satisfy
But you are more than this
My Love, you are the prize

-Oh, Love will carry the load
Let faith and hope take hold
Oh, love will carry the load
Faith and Hope forever show
There is more to love

Blue Eye Dream

A dream within a dream swept me off my feet
You and I appeared within an empty room
Love was not on hold for it became our speech
Our tongues were tied and twisted
Our lips perfectly in sync

I thought I'd never see you again
And then I soon awoke
And you were right beside me
We had never been apart

Fifty years together, you and I
It was beautiful to say the least
And then I awoke again
Alone beneath the sheets

Blue eyes within this dream
Yellow hair within that dream
A face of heaven's angel sent to me
And so, I believe in Love

206. The Day

The day will come
You'll rise up believing that you've won
So sets the sun
If we fall we rise up with our guns

Take my hand
Riding currents
Becoming the wind
I will see you around
If this world wants us to meet again

-Today is the Day
We celebrate all we have done
Man-made landscape
For us to love and to enjoy the world

207. $3.13

What is broke?
What number puts you at your lowest of lows?
One dollar or five
One penny for a fight

I give my love freely
To whomever I please
My passion not bound by ceilings
My hope busting through the seem

3.13 tells you who you should be
What could you buy with that change on the street?
But what good is change when you're thrown in jail
Living within metal isn't heaven or hell

This is silly
Rant, repeat, and conceal defeat
3.13

208. Give Thanks

Questioning everything creates a weary mind
And so I give thanks in these troubling times
Let go!

209. Without You

-These words mean nothing without you
This life seems empty without you
I am losing my mind little by little every night
Without you

If grace is gone don't give me the good news
When autumn frosts have slain July it is proof
And not even the seasons satisfy without you in my life
This old truth
Not even the songbirds sing it right without you in my life
Without you

My purpose is to please you my dear friend
I seem to have lost the will to fight again
You appear in my dreams and I wake in tears
This the curse of a lonely man
I feel you close so here I stand
Praying you will give me one more chance dear friend

210. Music City Blues

I worked the fields of Southern Ground
A sinful teenager just roamin'round
I broke the law and paid my dues
I fled to worship the Music City Blues
            I became Mr. CandyMan   avoiding God's big plan
            I became a lover and a long lost friend
To-wards a bitter end

I've broke some hearts and had my heart break too
And I've lived to learn the Music City Blues
            They say grass is green, but I can hear it blue

(Chorus)

So I return to the light I left many years ago
I am looking for love within these rabbit holes
            I come down South to pay my wicked dues
            But my God returned my heart and I have proof
I can sing Music City Blues

- I've taken many baby steps to be where I'm today
And I thank my God for giving me a second chance to say
Our God is great. Our God is Great

Indian Mounds

I ended up at double dogs watching a football game
Manchester United chasing Wolfsburg here at play
I sat down as my friends were outside finishing their cigarettes
And a stranger came up next to me yearning for a chat
He said, "Hey, my name is Randy and I am a regular double dog"
He smelled of boos, his shirt half tucked, and his shoelaces tied wrong
He asked me where I am from because my accent sounded "south"
I said, "Sir, I am from Georgia." Then Randy got real loud
He said,
"So you know about them Indian Mounds
With them spirits everywhere...?
I hear they make them dream catchers
Because of all the living dead
He spoke about some zombies walking around in the spooky state
I spoke of Stone Mountain, Dahlonega and Rattlesnakes
Now Randy was from LA. He has been in Music City awhile
He said his ex-wife drove him here
She is a whore who never smiles
He asked me why I was in Nash Vegas
And why I was hanging around these guys
I said I write songs just for fun and Randy got bug-eyed
He said,
I bet you must be good then
Georgia breeds that type all right
Many wonderful writers are bred below the Tennessee line
He then gave me a questionable grin
I thought he was about to stroke and die
And then he got real close and said,
"Hey friend, you want to know why?"
It is because of those God-damn Indian Mounds
I am telling you my friend
Those spirits come to speak and all you Georgia boys just listen
He swore by the name of Jesus they landed Alan Jackson success
He kept on counting names and I said,
"Randy, I must confess"
I am one half Native American; I have got Indian in my blood
I always hear them in my head
It is how I write my songs
He got real red and his mouth zipped up
I tried hard not to laugh
He softly whispered, "I knew it"
And asked the bartender for another glass
Thank God for all those Indian Mounds
Thank God for good company and loyal friends
I will never forget that coo-key old man
Who gave me a song to sing out loud
God bless them Georgia boys and those God-damn Indian Mounds

211. Oh God, How you Change

Oh God, how you change
You twist and turn and still remain
Your heart my God
Your heart is what I am drawn towards

People say the heart can change
But can it?
I guess so
But the heart can be known
Forever,
The seeds of the heart can be reaped and sewn
I do not know you
But, I wish to know you
I cannot speak on behalf for you
I pray you do not speak on behalf of me
I beckon let me learn you
I beckon let you learn me
I do not know you
But, I wish to know you

I pray, God show me the way
Show me your way
Keep me in your light
I need you now more than ever
This Love
Love me please
This Love
Love me still
This love heals me and guides me
Love me still.

212. Comeback to the Lord

Come
Come back to the Lord
He will be yours
      You will be mine
      You will be mine

Life is too short
To live it alone
I beg you come home
      I cannot do this alone
      I cannot do this alone

-I have found peace in these days
Though people may say
He is lost and afraid
He has got no sense in his brain

-I have no fear for today
I fear not trouble on the way
My Lord is here to stay
My Lord is here to stay
My Lord is here to stay

213. Prove to Me

My oh my, some time has gone by
I apologize if you have been compromised
I just wanted to drop in to check up and say Hi

Old friend, it has been awhile
I am a sinner trying out a new lifestyle
I am wasted. I am chasing. I am a fool
But my road has led to you
      Take me in with all my ways
      Prove to me that I can change

Lord, you have been playing some twisted games
To the world, I have become somebody strange
I am confused today and I do not know what to do
This road has led to you
      Take me in with all my way
      Prove to them that I can change
      Could the time I lost really be too long?
      To keep you from coming home?
      Could the time I lost really be too much?
      To steal you from my trust?

214. She Could Not Understand

She could not understand
The weight of the world
Too much to comprehend
And so she fades into dust
Seasons continue to change
The crust in her mind sheds
As tears then hit the ground

What was lost is now found
To come again, to save the day
And Jesus came
Water runs and turns to blood
The sun's light never fades
And Jesus came

What once was lost has now been found
To come again, to save the day
And Jesus came and Jesus came
The sun's light will never fade

She could not understand
This new power within her hands
And Jesus came and Jesus came
The sun's light will never fade

215. Depression

Depression the cart
Heavy the load
Wear the horses down
We won't make it home for Christmas

Forget the bread and drink the wine
Sell your shoes and shirt for one more pint
Wear the horses down and drive them off the road
We will not make it home this year for Christmas

Following the Course

The Years are short and the days are long
You will soon understand these words my son
God does not call the qualified
He qualifies the called
Find what is the word of God and live it
Those who claim they have absolute truth are false prophets
Follow the Course and let your passions never be satisfied
This will allow you to be driven all the way to the Promised Land

216. A Man's Answer to A Woman's Question
(For My Wife)

Do you understand I am the luckiest man?
Ever made by the great hand above?
Your beautiful heart, this beautiful life
With your wonderful womanly love!
> I know that I am asking for a priceless thing
> As a child would ask for a toy
> I want what others would die to win
> Your love for this patient young boy
I do not mean to put you out
I dare not question thee
I am ever so waiting at the door of your soul
Until you will come with me
> I do not require any meal hot
> Who needs clothes lest you are cold?
> My heart is as true as God's Stars
> As pure as His Heaven, my soul
I will slaughter only the fattest of cows
You will never need for a thing
Your seamstress skills are more than enough
And I will be your man and your King!
> And you will be Queen within this realm called home
> And a woman that the Maker, our God
> Shall look upon as he did on the first
> And say, "Damn, it is good!"
And though we are both young and like roses will fade
I long to kiss your lips and I pray
That soon we will both mellow 'neath mid fallen leaves
And reminisce of the month of May
> My heart is an ocean so strong and deep
> So, I launch my all on its tide
> You will discover there is a heaven on earth
> This day as you become my bride
I require all things grand and true
And all these things we will be
If you give me a chance I also will be
All that you demand of me
> I will always be this, a husband and father,
> And a pure light to lead the way
> My heart will forever beat in your chest
> For the remainder of our days
So come with me and we shall find good rest
By our Father near the brush
He will sanctify us for eternity
And in Heaven he'll dance for us
> Because of our love, he will dance for us!

217. <u>You're in My Head and my Heart</u>

You go child
You know you don't stay
There is more on the way
There is more than this hole you have dug
So get out and shake the rug

Over and over will fall the rain
Skies seemingly gray
There is no room for fun
When the sun' always on the run

Oh my head. OH!
You're in my head
You're in my head and my heart
Oh my heart. OH!
You're in my heart.
You're in my head and my heart

218. <u>Memory #6</u>

I am sliding head first down the stairs
In a red jacket
I am turning the corner soon to hear
A puppy in a cage

I wandered about the racket
And how those eyes did stare
We named her after Homeward Bound
Not the one who cut my hair!

Red Jacket worn down by green grass stains
Sliding head first down the hill
That same hill we would sled down
If Georgia forecast willed the snow

Some memories seem make believe
Maybe they all are
If so I am a lunatic
Writing these poems all alone

219. Forever I Apprentice (Mama Tried)

Forever I apprentice
Until my time is done
Forever worshipping the father
Giving glory to the son

Forever I apprentice
A disciple of many kinds
But first and foremost I disciple
The source, the holy, the divine

Forever I apprentice
Never meant to be the best
I will do my best to save the rest
I release my heart as I confess

Forever I apprentice
Sometime here, sometimes there
You walk with me all the daylong
You sing me hymns and choral song

Forever I apprentice
Under the big band in the sky
I am breathing the good word
And attempting to never lie

Forever I apprentice
As I am, so are you
We should live this life as one
You and I and me and you!

220. Long Days, Short Years

Every day that passes I recall what you once said
The days are long, the years are short, invest in a good bed!
Every day that passes I dream much weirder dreams
Sometimes I am a hero and sometimes a great villain!
Every day that passes I seem to drift father away
My soul gets closer to Heaven and my heart longs for that day!
Every day that passes I again wish for your love
I want you more today than ever before
My God, My Lord, My Love

Faith, Hope, Love

I am up past my bedtime
Printing and Burning
Printing and Burning
One more day of this until I can rest
Four days of rest
More than enough to find balance in you
Balance this crazy life
Sleep less, Work more
I write to record
I write for you and for me
To remember
To Understand
To be a disciple
To attempt to disciple

I have faith in this Love
I hope you will understand this Love
I Love you so much!

221. I Am Sleepy

Can a poem be rushed?
Some I write slowly, and some I write fast
I am tired and am not worried
This will soon be a thing of the past

I reread some poems and think I am mad
It is funny to see what things make me sad
Reflecting on life for personal gain
To conquer emotion daily is the game

So pick up your cross and walk this way
There is no more time to waste for we cannot stay here

222. Savior, Save Me (Revised)

It was supposed to be me
All by myself
Walking over to the Turnip Truck
Yet, you were right beside me
Coming in my head and my heart just to see what's up
I sank into deep thought
Wandering why you'd choose me to play this part
And so I carried on along, loving every second,
Keeping all the lights turned on

-I remember thinking,
"If there is a savior...
Then save me!"

In a hot cave all day
My blood is boiling, I am praying for a change
And here you come again
Saying, "Peace be with you. You know I am always here"
I sank into deep thought
Lord, why choose me to play this part?
I carried on along, loving every second,
Keeping all the lights turned on

-I remember screaming in my soul
Savior! Save ME

223. I'm A Dog

I am not the best at tableside
And I've told my share of lies
I've dug in dirt a time or two
I'm good at drinking wine
I am good at waiting patiently
If I feel like being nice
Meatloaf tempts me
As does a fat ole cheesecake slice

-Cuz I'm a dog
A fuggin' dog
I chase my tale
I never fail to know where I went wrong
Cuz I'm a dog
A fuggin' dog
D.O.G. The only me
Every livelong daylong

I piss all over couches
If I do not get my way
I bark at any simpleton
I bark at the fireplace
I am always in your corner
I am a true and bestest friend
Keep me in mind, one of a kind
With loving wet kisses

224. Broadway

You can hear every band simultaneously
As you walk along Broadway
Just nod your head
As excellence sweeps across your soul
As your heading our way

I hear people making noise
From twelfth south to Fifteenth Avenue
The world is shaking and of course it's true
You got me and I got you

Could you let forty days go by without her in your arms?
Cuz I don't think so

225. January 1st

I hear that a good writer only writes
If he has something revolutionary to say
Or if he can think of a way
To say something new

And so I listen carefully
I continue to write nonstop
Some work is planned and other work is not
I just write and write and write

The first person I see is also my first friend
Once when I came back and another when I return
They play the parts of Game of Thrones
They sing and dance and are merry

These people are familiar and also family
Even the strangers are familiar and I consider them friends
I am blessed to have all I need to succeed
I think of my past
I think of all of my friends
I think of all of my future friends
I am so excited to be alive

Every day that goes by I am happier
I am closer to you and to everything
I am excited to further critique myself
Forever and ever evolve to be better
To get closer to you
To be one with you

I consider my faults
I consider that I have faults that I am not aware of
I pray these will be brought to light so I may fix them
I am aware I cannot fix everything
This does not discourage me
This makes me want to fight harder
This encourages me to work harder
To network better
To be better
I am the past, present, and future.
I am the best me there can be

This year I put myself at the altar
This year I step foot in the light
This year I begin pouring my spiritual foundation
For now, and forever
I hold fast to you Lord as I fast for you
        This is my life work
        To worship and bring balance to those in need
        Through worship I will exalt your name
        Through worship I will bring this city together
        Through worship I will teach about the foundation
        Through worship I will become a better disciple
        Through interdisciplinary studies
        I reveal God to the world
        I will show every brother the shape of the Lord
        The shape of life and love
        From the Genesis Pattern to the Heart of David
        This will be the beginning

And so, I sit here with two years of games, two years of life in Nashville, and two years working on Home's Farm. The seventh year brings luck. This is promised to me. I have found my love sitting 'neath the Redding Tree. The Redding Tree soon becomes again the Wedding Tree as my mind begins to focus towards better days and grandeur things.

I have changed in many ways. I am grateful for every spirit that has graced me to this day. I want to be a light to these people who have given me light and life freely. I work hard every day for the hope of becoming who I know I can be. I understand I will never catch up to that man, but I know that with perseverance I can overcome any obstacle, as long as I am surrounded by people that I love, and who love me.

I roam around this ground with memories of an undeveloped piece of land. Now, I see the beginning of something wonderful and powerful. A great healing ground. A great place for many men and women to learn and grow. And they will pour in by the hundreds of thousands for over a hundred years!

End

PART THREE (B)... Joshua and the Spirit of Moses

Peace During War

It took one hour for my heart to shatter
It took a year to repair it
It will take another year to build up strength
It will take another year to get used to it
It took one hour for my heart to shatter
War has begun!
I pray for peace and for guidance
Her picture is within arm's reach
Her soul is an eternity away
I can barely hear her voice
It fades... as the dream fades
Lord, give me peace in this time of war!

226. Jam

Jam
Nothing gets me moving like good rhythm
Swaying and spicing up the mood
Settling into a beloved groove
There is nothing in this world quite like
Jam
Nothing gets me moving like good music
Swaying to the beat and up the groove
Settling into heavenly mood
There is nothing in this world quite like Jam

227. The Devil Song

See I am the Devil
Fool of selfish pride and selfish hate
See I am the problem
No one can escape the beauty of my fate
My lovely angel wings
My lovely gift from God
Come and see
I'll bring you in to everything
Come into my world
Won't you come with me?

228. Coming from the Backwoods

Coming from the backwoods
I came up on a do
She stared at me as if I was a headlight
As it began to snow

-It made me think of Nashville
Which used to be my home
Until the Good Lord said,
"It's time for you to go!"

Coming from the backwoods
I tried to understand
How I could fit the city
Being from the country land?

-Then I remembered Fayetteville
Welcoming me with open arms
Until I heard the Good Lord say,
"I'll be your lucky charm!"

Doot toot a lootle toot
Dootle mmm doo doo doo

229. Towards the End of the Day

Towards the end of the day
The mist of darkness rolls through the hills
The lark songs begins to sing in tune
As the symphony relaying God's Will

The sound of music cascading as water
Falling from the heights of cliffs in waves
The push and pull is war on gravity
As we reach towards the sky for grace

May the birds
May the bees
All bugs
Every breeze
Chorally sing and proclaim
How amazing you are

May the elements proclaim
One single name
In awe of how great you are.

230. Poetry and Purpose

I am not the world's best poet
I hardly even rhyme
But I write from the heart
All of the time
Sometimes it is more than words
I try to match up
It is what I think I need to read
When I am down and casted out
For the world does not accept
People like me
They spit and curse and thrash us
They laugh when we bleed
But I do not care about that
I have my God upon my side
I worship him and him alone
No idol will become my prize

The first poem turned to song
Lullaby
How appropriate!
An atheist saved by Jesus
A writer turned to the Lord
A life dedicated towards evangelism
A modern time Paul
Relatable and wise
Create a world my son!
Do not get caught in fiction,
But dwell in the fantasy!

231. We Don't Need This No More

Why don't you say what you mean?
Why don't you mean what you say?

-Lady, just come away with me
Because we don't need this no more
Baby, sail away with me
Honey we don't need this no more

I'm gonna show you how
We're gonna run this town
This man will flip you upside down
That's fo sho
Girl you listen up
This gonna funk you up
We gonna rock this boat all night

-Lady, just come away with me
Because we don't need this no more
Baby, sail away with me
Honey we don't need this no more

They see you walking around
You are the talk of the town
You are woman that is gonna wanna man
To step up and get laid
You are the pedestal
And you are all that is good
I swear we are gonna leave
And we won't care about what other people say

232. Just to be Alone with You

I would give up everything just to be alone with you
I would sail across the Milky Way just to be alone with you
I'd easily give up forty days of my life
To be alone with you

233. I'm Still a Fool

If you would let me
          I would be your fool
Whatever you'd need!
          Darling, I'd be cool
You are essential to me
          Not a day goes by
Where I do not think of you
          Our lips intertwined
I am still a fool for you

-When everything is okay
          We are laughing
And every summer day
          We are dancing

234. We Will Meet Again

I burnt the bridge; I fell in the trap
I stumbled towards the mirror
I shattered the man inside the glass
To free him from the terror

I sought the sheep and fought to keep
My morals so not to waste them
For many will die to keep these safe
So love meets to unfold him

-I count down every single day
Knowing we will meet again
Whether introduced as friends
Or falling face down in the sand
On Heaven's shores
Don't be alarmed my love is yours

And so I come and so I weep
I never knew behooving
And so I sit in the loser's seat
Yet, her love seeks better loving

-I count down every single day
Knowing we will meet again
Whether introduced as friends
Or falling face down in the sand
On Heaven's shores
Don't be alarmed my love is yours

235. The Dream that Stopped my Heart

I was running in a field.
I was running as fast as I could.
She was on the other side.
No progress made, but I keep running towards her.
I am trying so hard.

All of the sudden she sees me.
She sees how hard I am running.
She sees how hard I am trying.
This is usually when the dream ends.

Last night she took that step
She came towards me. It was the final step.
All of the running. The trying.
The many failed attempts.
It took her just one step to reach me.
And we collided.

We passionately kissed and made love until the sun rose.
And then I awoke. Alone

The Gift on the Night Stand

A gift from you to lift my heart
A replica of my guitar
Fabricated as a box
Free to open, free from locks
You kissed me as you grasped my hand
I place the gift on the night stand

236. You Got it, You

There lived a man before those skeleton eyes sank in
You got it, you got it, you got it, you
There was a woman who lost her soul there too
You got it, you got it, you got it, you
       I was behaving the best I could
       She was behaving the best she could
       I was behaving the best I could
       If she only knew

-I close my eyes and see blue fire falling like rain
I close my eyes and see new colors on every face

237. Keep Going

I walked into the next room to see if she was still alive
She was scorning me creating lies within her mind
I fought so hard and still lost the battle and the war
I found my body sore and every piece of my heart torn

I invited her to the breakfast table she seemed so confused
She never loved me anyways I was something to amuse her
So I went to the good Lord, He said there is more to life
And so I packed my bags, said my goodbyes
        And then prepped for my flight
        She was in her own world too
        She had her sister pick her up
        An evil woman full of bitterness and bad luck

-AND this life can get pretty rough
All I can say is keep on going
Keep Going, Keep Going
This life can beat you up
So find yourself some aspirations
And Keep Going, Keep Going

238. She Came from Salem

She would not, could not compare
She is nothing
Hawthorne could not capture such despair
She is something

As I continue to connect the bridges
I understand to my demise
In their eyes, I was equivalent to a witch
I was neither lucky nor wise

I continued to play my game
They continued to play theirs
I fought so hard and lost the battle
Yet, the war remains up in the air

She came from Salem
A descendant of John
She is now my curse
And so I fled from her arms

I thank God every day that I came back to the farm. My heart still aches for the love that I lost. I never thought I would be able to feel again, but I am learning about this woman and she is turning the wheels in my heart. She is only to be a friend. She is only to be close from a distance because my walls remain up. I have yet to rid myself of her picture in my desk. It is so hard to write openly and confess.

I keep the keychain she gifted me. I have yet to let go of the love for my lady. I truly thought her as my wife. The Lord prevented such perverted ties. I was meant for someone else. A greater woman and nothing less. May I have found this woman already? Only a year has gone past since I lost my lady. A woman now stands to my left and she is beautiful. Another woman is entering the room from the right and she is also beautiful. Regardless of the outcome I will be a happy man and I will live this life with no regrets the best I can. I know the woman who is meant for me will satisfy my needs in every way and I will lean on her strength when I am weak until judgement day.

239. Young Man

Dearest young man,
You know not me; I know not you
Yet we are connected through and through
You know not me; I know not you
Yet we are kin as sky and ocean are blue
            He replies with a smirk
            That analogy will not work
            For I hear the color amongst the sky
            It is neither blue nor purple (his soliloquy)
            And the ocean she sings
            There is red and black and yellow
Dearest young man,
Do not cast such thought into the world
Color is something you see
            His shadow casts an echo
            Color is something you feel
            It is something to taste
            Something that is real
Dearest young man,
Do not be a fool
For a fool lines his life with struggle and strife
Color is a sense for the eyes
            But the eyes are the source for most lies
            Though the window to the soul
            The eyes can be tented and shine false glow
            And so twenty-two and I am tired

Dearest young man,
Continue the course and understand
I am a friend, beaten by life
I can no longer walk and my back will not let me ride
I have seen many things and in time you will see
Color is a whore of a thing

She is blessed
She is an angel here upon this earth
After a single night with her
I cling to her skirt and I whisper
Love, I will follow you to Heaven
And so she laughed in irony
For he did not know her plan
To drain him, to use him, to abuse him
She is blessed

You, so blessed, do not see truth
Do you not understand our sin?
Do you not see the sin of man whole and equal?
The man behind the pulpit holds the same weight
As the murdering rapist lurking the streets of Athens!
This is the truth. Righteous or not!
The difference between a righteous man and a sinful man
Is not location?
Tis the matter at which one chooses to live daily
Are you pursing truth and purity?
It is not for me to judge for it is the Lord who judges
And our good Lord will judge the heart
And so I pray for eyes
I pray for wisdom of the mind so I may have strong eyes
Lord, let me see the heart of man individually and as the whole
How black is our heart? How pure is the heart of Christ truly?

240. Living in a Dream within a Dream

Look above, touch the stars, feel the love
I took a chance tonight
I caught the flight to be with you again
Let's huddle up, a love riot, ride chariots
I took a chance, got up to dance, and we began

The Giant Diamond
Speak the truth, speak of life
Live and learn and love
Life is proof and pure as white
Give and serve and love

241. The Lost Boy Died

The lost boy died
A man surfaced to replace the weak
The spirit came to guide the meek
Though the lost boy tried

The man will not fail
The man is backed by the Lord
The boy bestowed by innocence
The man falls to the sword.

The lost boy died today.

242. Super Monkey

I promised to write about him
Super Monkey
Hours spent on him
Studying Super Monkey
Days spent watching him
Studying Super Monkey
What is the reason for him?
Letting go of Super Monkey

How can I continue to babble when there are souls waiting to be saved? Is it to grab the attention of someone who need randomized stimulation? This is possible. Out of the several billion people in the world I am confident that there are many people out there like me. I know that there are many people waiting to get lost in the world of chaos to find more order than in the outside world. We crave the virtual experience.

243. The List

Some poems are not meant to rhyme
I write nonsense all the time
These experiences are mostly freeform
Each experience as unique as a storm
Each experience within a new day
Each experience told in a new way
I pray you have guidance and pursue only truth
I hope the transitions of life remain smooth

I wrote out a list of significant themes

How could Jesus be God? God has no history. If God is omnipresent than how is man free? The solution brought about by C.S. Lewis suggests that it is because God sits outside of time. Man exists in the linear realm of time. God sees this line of time as a whole. Man has a beginning and man has an end while God does not.

God places himself in the perfect time for his story to make the biggest impact. Is it not strange that we base our time off the life of Jesus? Jesus could easily be debated as the most famous person in human history. I have been in illusion that God can foresee my actions. I have been assuming that my life is predestined because I have forgotten that the Lord blessed me with choice. The Lord blesses every human being with choice. Daily, we are able to act upon how we want to exercise our free will. We can do it as a slave or we can do it as a free man despite our circumstances.

I forget that God stands outside of time. He is not bound by linear action as man is. When I sinned yesterday the Lord saw me sinning. When I sinned today it was not as if he forgot or even has to remember me sinning because he just sees me in the process of sinning. If I were to repeat the same sin tomorrow it would be no different from the day before. The Lord would see me sinning in the present simultaneously as he did yesterday and the day before. These are big ideas and are full of compounding truth.

God does not foresee my sin because he is there in the present as I am sinning. Whether it was a year ago or a year from now God is with me the same. Today I feel his presence and I am aware of his grace, mercy, and love. If I do not feel it the same way tomorrow or next year the grace, mercy, and love will still be the same but it will be me that is disconnected. I pray that I can remain in a constant state of worship through the remainder of my days because it is the most important thing to me. Growth and Health hold strong as principle, but worship is essential for eternal health.

The God that I serve is Love, yet he is so much more. The God I serve is above time itself. The God I know possesses power far greater than time and the devil can comprehend. Mortality leads to death, but my Heart in Jesus is everlasting. The immortality of God is irrational and the more we try to rationalize it the more we diminish the inspiring awe of the Lord.

When pondering if Jesus is God I reflect on the idea of God's omnipresence. When considering the trinity, I imagine a child. I imagine my child. At the time of closing my eyes as soon as I elect through my will to imagine a child he immediately spawns. The act of God imagining his son as being the savior and the bridge is what allowed Jesus to be the savior and the bride. This is why Jesus was able to assume his fate amongst his people with such accuracy. The act of God's Will has always been producing the mental image of Jesus and Holy Spirit as a unit. God is love and love works through men.

Let us reflect on the Holy Spirit in terms of a company and its people. You have a creator who sparks a vision of excellence. You have people who follow in the image of that creator pursuing towards the created vision. And then, you have the spirit of the collected group on how it impacts the world outside of the company. When an outsider enters the realm of this company are they going to be drawn to this spirit, or are they going to sense evil and despair. Are they going to sense growth, or are they going to see a company in decline?

244. Heavenly Euphoria

An overwhelming experience
A Holy Spirit experiment
The link between the generations
The bridge imagined before creation

The world before the time did come
The world before the rising sun
The mist that poured out over all
The few who answered the mighty call

A near death experience
Is this the only source for "spiritual awakening"?
When people are at their lowest of lows
Is this the moment of reckoning?

245. Divine Intervention

This is the perfect moment
When everything in the Universe leads up to this
That split second when you cannot miss
This is that perfect moment

I sit in the front row
This is Divine Intervention
I see him approaching me
I sit in the front row

He calls me by name
I reply in greetings
He reveals himself as Joshua
He calls me by name

He handed me a letter
I read it and shivered
I ran far away
When he handed me that letter

Saved through Music

A doctor with religious opinion
He studies Eastern Philosophy
He believes he has been saved...
Through music

Mozart believed it came from Heaven
I am talking of music
King David believed it came from God
I am talking of Music
Jesus worshipped through his work
I am talking about music
Paul wrote letters that changed the world
I am still talking about music

246. Pain is Temporary

To be a coward is the most dangerous way to live
To be courageous is the safest way to live
This is reference to the Christian way of life
The philosophy of Christianity is serious and admirable.

"Pain is temporary" says the Lord
I believe Jesus thought this
Over and over and over
Many a man through history
Pain is temporary

The Lord will not let a sleeping dog lie. Bad temper and drunkenness spoil the pureness of daily life. Putting yourself in the hand of the Lord will place you in the pursuit of perfection. Daily growth and constant chase towards a blameless life. God is easily to please, but very hard to satisfy and this is because of his omnipresence. Every moment in time is the present to him. Every moment since the dawn of time and every moment until the end of time is the present to our infinite God.

When you begin by writing about yourself you lose the importance of life. When you get lost in your own self you will lose the complete purpose of what it means to be human. Even the ordinary man will become extraordinary when he realizes what the purpose is. The purpose is God. The purpose is assuming his Will upon your life. The purpose is exposing yourself to selflessness so one can push away the bad habits to make room for newer and better habits. Let the Lord force your spirit to a higher level of consciousness.

247. Decisions

What is the purpose?
I don't believe I can fly anymore
I will never spawn wings
Regardless, I have a mind

I believe I can fly
I can imagine my wings
In time I will construct them
The Lord has given me a mind

And so we study the drama of scripture
It is revealed in pieces through a strange mixture
Each person takes what they will
Each person will eat their fill

Christianity is a beautiful philosophy
Patriotism is a dangerous religion
Fear and shame quickly lead to idolatry
May the Lord reveal to you this Holy vision

These collected books are clippings of God
These collected poems are heavenly songs
Written in the Spirit and sang in love
Given through the angels sent from above

248. Why You Dreaming?

Why are you dreaming?
Don't go to sleep yet
Why are you talking loud?
There is nothing to talk about
Why are you walking out?
Don't you leave just yet
I've got so much to show you
Hidden deep in my chest
            -Is this okay?
            Is this alright?
Why are you falling away?
Can you not hear my prayers?
Why don't you walk with me for a while?
We can stare at the stars
The table is set for us two
Me and You
I have the oldest of wine
Lucky you

249. The Love Song from Long Ago

And sings my soul
I am strangely inspired
I since her growing closer

Her body shaped to perfection
And then her counterpart
They could not be more opposite

The fruit forebears love
This love is real
As artificial intelligence surfaces
This love is real

She does not know me
She wishes to know me
I wish to know her
On my own terms

She does not know me
She wishes to know me
I should not judge her
I should learn her

I know what I want
Yet she wishes to know me
I wish to know her
If she is patient enough

      Why is it that David was so inspired? Why is it that Solomon was so inspired? It is easier to understand the mind of the second generation because of the clear inspiration deriving from the first generation. I get to witness history repeat itself in an incredible way. The stakes appear to be much higher because it is I who am experiencing it. This is not to take away from the severity of any previous generation. I just acknowledge that I indeed am witnessing the cycle Historical Overturn.

250. Her Name

Her name is alluring and wants me to glance
Her ways are so moving it makes my feet dance
Her glow is so new to me I want to look
Her body is magical as wizardry books

Her name is the Pure Pearl.

The sixth message is important because it is the second to last message in this book. It is the heaviest message. It is the last sign before the cliff itself. It is the cock of the gun before the trigger is pulled. The intensity of this message cannot be forgotten.

I have not been writing as frequent. I have allowed life to get in the way between me and my other passions. It is funny how life makes you want. I want to learn daily, I want experience, I want everything to be brand new all of the time... and these desires are leading me to become someone who is insatiable.

Now, I have been learning new styles of writing. I am learning to remove myself from the center of my own self. I am thinking back to all of the things I have read, and I am considering all of the people that I have written with in the past. I am imagining all of the faces of the dozens of people who have helped me write these hundreds of songs, and I am imagining the hundreds of people who helped create these hundreds of stories. This is just a microscopic sample on the crust of a world that can offer so much more than I will ever know.

There is so much good in this world, but there is still so much evil. There is light, yet so much darkness. It seems for every accomplishment there are ten judgments. This is the world today. The world today is a beautiful place if you know how to explore it with people you mean to explore.

Conviction

When the body no longer feels conviction
How could I be so deaf to the voice of God?
How could I be so numb to sin?
Is it because the pleasure exceeds the conviction?
The momentary pleasures of Life

I feel conviction
It is strange where it comes up
I am numb to some sin and keen towards others
I pray to not repeat the past
Life is full of struggle and darkness
You will make mistakes
Do not make the same mistake twice!
If you do, repent!
The Kingdom of Heaven is at hand!
The time is now. The fruit is ripe.

Feel conviction Israel!
Feel conviction doers of wrong.
The beast cannot feel conviction
The beast refuses to feel
The beast consumes
The thief will be riding on its back

251. Rags

I wear rags.
Every day I put on my rags and go to work
I wear black
Every day I reflect on the shadows of the past
I stare back
Every day I reflect on the last
I wear rags
Every day I push forward never forgetting my past
To build, to grow, to learn, to love
I get one life… I am going to live it to the fullest.

252. The Day I Met Her

Here I am on the brink of insanity
I was lost in the workforce
I traded my rags for a pretty penny
And lay naked on the floor

Here I am tossing and turning at night
Her memory is casting shadows on the wall
I aim my arrow ready to fight
The prophecy reads that cupid will fall

Here I am cursing her name
Cursing the day I met her
She will soon bring me autonomous fame
To this day I am removing the burrs

Finally, the wounds have all healed
A new war is approaching
I have spent a year fasting as I kneeled
As her army was nautically boasting

253. The Beauty of the Night

My favorite words to speak as she walks
My favorite phrase to use as she talks
I will never assume a place in her bed
"You take my breath" is what she said
       Cast your lines in meter and rhyme
       Fake the love from time to time
       "Come to me and you will find rest"
       She pressed her chest against my chest
She gave her best, I gave my best
We lost our way and found our place
Away from the world to take the test
Until we meet again face to face
       "I will not forgive you" she would say
       I wanted to love her till our hairs turned grey
       She could not keep me, nor I keep her
       The earth keeps spinning as we shift to dirt
You allowed him to come and take my place
A different day, a different face
I could not attempt to change this world
I fell in love with a girly girl
       It gets better than this I must admit
       Her love was something I could not quit
       I lost my way and threw away my name
       I took the role of the Devil's game.

254. North Point on the Southside

> LifePoint, CrossPoint, North Point, Southside
> Free Chapel, Passion City, the Fellowship Collide
> I twist and turn, I reap and sew
> I am losing my sweet mind
> I do not recall you coming in
> I was playing guitar inside

Will Durant would not have words to describe the shape of the new world
Is this the world we were taught about in Sunday School?
Is this the type of world that I would want to raise children in?
I question these things in vigor.
We exist in a form of purgatory, this abeyance of spiritual suspension, as we
wait for the future to reveal a light that is in each one of us.
People expect a catalyst to guide us to Heaven while some people believe
the we exist in a time represented as the aftermath of this catalyst. This new
age is seen as the common era.
Yet, we exist in a whole new timeline. Year 16. Luxury that will not stand the
test of time. Lifestyles that will not extend past a single generation. The
selected few will have a chance to leave a mark on this world, so will they
pursue this in an egotistical manner, or will the step up in selflessness. My
brother, do not lock the door and throw away the key during this time.
Am I evil? Am I the sin that keeps us from the light? In my attempt to
discover the light for myself am I pushing more and more away from said
light? This paradox, this push and pull of emotion and self-worth is enough
to drive any man insane. I admit, it has driven me to the cliff's edge on
multiple occasions.

Embarrassingly enough I have not been with a woman in eight months. This
is this longest I have gone without sexual relations since I was fourteen
years old and I have noticed that my hedonistic lifestyle has increased
steadily since that time. By keeping myself from the desires of the flesh I
have been compensating through other measures. I have been avoiding
sobriety and I have been avoiding good health in attempts to fill that void of
sexual immorality. Does this make any sense?

Yes, I do not have to worry about pregnancy, STD, or sustaining unhealthy
relationships tied together by the powerful strings of premarital sex, but I
am forced to deal with the loneliness of being single. I do not hesitate to say
that the peace I have found during this time has laid a strong foundation for
self-improvement which will benefit me in the long run, but now I have to
decide to actually execute this lifestyle. I will dedicate myself to work,
practice, and growth.

I know that these seeds will only bear the purest of fruit. I want to learn how to truly put God first. I need to understand first, who God truly is. I have many ideas, but these are only my perspective. I continue to describe the Heart of David as the most accurate philosophy for self-help, self-improvement, spiritual awakening, self-awareness, and humanitarianism.

I don't have to have a thing

255. The Days that Roll

Good days, bad days
Long days, short days
Some days I am afraid
In some ways I have not changed

Your strength is all I need
I need you to believe in me
I will not succeed for in this soil I am weak
Your faith in me is all I seek

I pray the same prayers
I ride the same roads
I process the same tree
I process and then reload

Reboot my computer
Make me faster than ever
Make me better than ever
Rid the fog, make me clever

Fix the lamp and burn the oil
Break the straw as the water boils
Meal after meal and trail after trail
I am sick of the circles and I am sick of this world

Happiness is real and so is this love
Yet I find myself alone and in my head
This life is surreal as my best friend calls
I answer and we talk of faith, hope, and love

I bury my past and I look to the future
I exercise my free will towards work
I work towards the vision
I deny the dead ends when I approach the fork

We are champions in this time
Never forget where you came from
We will unite in confluence with the Lord's sign
Fray from the broad path leading against the horizon

Seek the blue and the gold
See them merge into one
Seek the honest and the bold
Yet, do not forget to have fun

The city is spoiled with flesh and rum
The countryside mourns the fallen sun
The conservative laughs and drinks his coffee
The liberal provides the excuse for her napping

Wake up and clean yourself!
Are you done here?
If you are not, then continue on
If you are then please come home

Life is too short to dwell incomplete
I long for the day when our two souls meet
You two and us two
She in your arms and her in mine

Our children in the fields
Our houses on the hills
We meet at the dining hall
We cook endlessly in thrill

Maybe they will dance for us
Maybe we will laugh as children
Maybe the dream will be all day
Maybe the dream will all remain

I must admit, I will never be satisfied
I will never quit
There is too much life to live
I will never stop

One by one and two by two
We will bring it together because I love you
One by one and two by two
We will bring it together because I love you

Random

She did curse me on the leave
I wrote this line before
I continue to write because I am unafraid
I am not scared of what they will find out
This is the age of recorded history
The truth will always be found out
We remain sinners, even today
Mankind has not shifted, not changed
We are the same
Do not claim to be more than you are
This is great, but it is not enough
The world is a big place and we are a small part of it
We are so minuscule compared to the world out there
I wish I had the proper words to do it justice but I do not
I am but an average man with an average vocabulary and that is okay
I cannot be something I am not, but I do have a strong passion for writing
There is something about formulating words on a page that makes me feel
alive

I get such a powerful rush by speaking what I feel God wants me to say
God... Just a word... Yet I truly hope you understand what I mean when I use
this word. I am simply not smart enough to prove the Lord's existence to any
and every man. And I simply do not have the clean slate to fall back on so one
could call me blameless or even selfless. I am a man. I am a musician. I am an
artist in my own way and I am full of love. I am overflowing with this love and
all I want to do is share it, but sometime I do not know how. I get consumed in
myself sometimes and I forget what to do. I let my anxieties and worries lead
me to bad habits that I repeat as a broken record left on overnight. Night after
night and day after day it plays on and on and on with no end. I might break
the record player but it is behind bulletproof glass and the speaker are out of
reach. This is utter annoyance. This is okay though. I am human and these
things truly are normal. Forms of pain, forms of depression, a lack of
understanding are all things every single human struggles with. Few voice it,
few acknowledge its existence for fear of being weak, but I know that I am
strong. I know that I am home.

256. Funny, Funny

I drink pinot noir
I watch my dog chew on a bone
He emits the worst aroma
Causation... Caesar's Cheese
I drink camel branded water
I think of my ferrets running around
Their glands radiate musky perfume
Causation... Enclosed cage
Rain patters on the painted deck
Tis the season of independence
Yet we are more dependent than ever
Oh how Rome will fall
Yet, we will always rise from the ashes
As the phoenix sings her song
Red Wine, Wet Rain
Summer smells midst cascades
The heat from the streets
The frozen red meats
The frozen white meats
The frozen blue berries
The constant rain
Funny, funny

An Excerpt from Victor Wooten's, "The Music Lesson"

Every time you move, and every time you play a note, a piece of yourself is
left behind.
Notes. Articulation. Technique. Feel. Dynamics. Rhythm. Tone. Phrasing.
Space. Listening.
Ossify- to become or turn into bone

Note- to notice or pay attention to, to say or write
Articulation- the action, state, or manner of being jointed or interrelated.
Technique- Using special skills or knowledge to perform
Feel- to be aware, to touch, to find
Dynamics- a pattern or process of change, growth, or activity
Rhythm- A regular repeated pattern of sounds, movements, events, changes,
and or activities
Tone- the quality in which one communicates
Phrasing- the way or the order in which something is expressed
Space- distance, area, volume, equality of separation
Listening- to hear the truth

I believe there is another very important element to add to this amazing list
of musical vocabulary and it would be to Adapt!

Adapt- to modify or fit in to any situation physically, mentally, socially, emotionally, and spiritually

Recognize the funny elements that make music worth listening to.

Victor speaks of Indian mounds, Nashville, and his spirit guides that showed him the path to spiritual awakening through worship in its purest form.

257. Rolling with Jacob

Rolling
We do not have any money
We are simply running errands
Rolling
We are searching
Diving in deep
We are Searching
And Rolling
I am rolling with Jacob
He is one of three
We all have the same idea
We are all rolling

258. North Carolina

Driving to Nashville
It had been a whole year
I saw the city sky line
I knew my family was near
The old familiar bars
The old familiar streets
The lure of all those city lights
The lure of everything

But she could not compare
To the mountainous air
Of North Carolina
Of North Carolina

I drove east through Tennessee
The long familiar road
I drove east through Knoxville
Another home away from homes

I miss my sweet home Nashville
But I love my new found home
Oh, the mountains of North Carolina
Those hills I love to roam

259. Returning to Green Hills

Sure a few more days' have past
This is nothing compared to a year
One whole year, nose to the grind
Working and shedding tears

Sure a few more days have past
A few days is nothing to me
Throw in a couple of weeks of work
A couple of months don't mean a thing

Sure a few more days have past
I passed through and it did not seem real
I saw long lost friends and family
Returning to Green Hills

Sure a few more days have passed
Georgia through Tennessee
Tennessee through North Carolina
North Carolina towards a dream

I admit this dream is not mine
I am a part of another man's vision
Until I can build my own dream up
For now, my dream is distant

For now, I sit in a class about science
The science of how we are made
I dream about Autumn Leaves falling
I dream about love and change

Every day that passes I believe
Life becomes more of a dream
Things are no longer what they seem
I am slowly building up a strong team

Together we dream about marching
We dream of singing a playing along
We dream about playing in California
We dream about the sea singing our song

260. The Return to Ducktown, TN

That Autumn breeze remains
You may not remember
I may have still been sane
How It rained last November
I never did complain
It brought up many questions
It brought up everything

Kolt and I wrote Baby Please
We set out for Chattanooga, TN
We played around the SEC
We sat back and prepared for 2017

Well, it was almost a year ago as I add onto this random piece of a poem. I never want to forget where I came from, or the road that I had to take to get where I am today. I am alive and I thank God every day. I should not be alive today after all of the evil I have committed, Yet, the Lord keeps me alive to this day.

How Did It Feel?
It felt great
It was amazing
It was a blurry weekend
Full of drinking and playing music with my friends
We had a good turnout
They left
It was okay
We had more fun without them

261. <u>Sunshine Part One</u>

Maybe we can sit around the fire
Pass the bowl all night
Just you and me drinking wine
Just you and me drinking all night
You and me sipping on gin, then wine

Drinking wine

I count down the days
Until I can see your face
You are my sunshine
My only sunshine
You make me happy
On a cloudy day
So I count down the days
Until I can see your face again
I count down the days
Until I can see your face
Till I can see your face

Sitting outside
And the fire is bright
One day, we are sipping on gin
And the next day wine
I said you are my sunshine
My only sunshine
You make me happy
On a cloudy day

Oh, I count the days

The snow outside
The fire is nice
Cut that Christmas Tree down
Bring that bitch inside
You are my sunshine
And this winter gets so cold
You are the Lark's Song when she sings,
"Calling me Home"

262. <u>Sunshine Part Two</u>

"Got some smoke in your eyes?
Maybe that isn't a good goal?"-Kolt
You radioed it in
As we were drinking gin
I saw that snow outside
Couldn't get you off my mind
She said you are like my home
So down deep inside
How the day turns to night?
When I got you by my side?
She said that fire is bright
I mean, the fire in your soul.
Every day when I'm with you
I never let go
She said this much, "I love you"
That moment I understood
The smell of her perfume
Makes me feel so good
And I said this much, "I Love you,
And I think about you all the time
I wouldn't dare to let you go now
I swear, it's getting mighty cold outside
So have a safe drive
I will see you very soon
I swear I never let go
Knowing this love is true"
And she said this much, "I love you"
And I think about you all the time
I see that fire in your eyes
And I know you are my sunshine

263. <u>Hebrews</u>

All day
      Work like Jesus
Every night
      Dance like David
When alone
      Write like Moses
STAND UP AND SWING

All day, walk the narrow
Every night, pray to the Lord
When alone, thank the Lord
STAND UP AND SING

My God, Bread and Life
My God, my morning star
My God, the Lark's song
Calling me home

Stand up and swing
Stand up and sing
Hill-top or low
Always calling me home

264. Panther's Creek

Panther's Creek
Tri-State Blues
Brown Hair, Brown Eyes
Or were they blue?
Or did she have blonde hair?
Or did we not hike?
Were we even camping?
Did we journey on bike?
I cannot recall
These memories aren't small
It is one too many lovers
Each plastered on a wall
They just take up space
Each proclaiming a place
My memories make faint
Of this man far from saint
Yet I climb this sobering hill
On up towards Calvary
Where he was hung
And he still loved me
And so he rose
And planted seeds
And like a rose
Covered in red
Conquering death
For you and me

265. One of Many, Many for One

Four long years studying the Bible
Do I ever cross your mind?
Am I a soldier in the History books?
Or a small face within the crowd?

Will I fade into nothing, with nothing left behind?
I hear it is wise to understand
We were made to pass on our knowledge
I have planted many seeds and there are many rows to go
Some are budding with little green leaves

Oh Lord, do not let me harden my heart
I have seen so little, and I yearn for each corner of this earth
Keep me still
The music is starting to play again
The music in my head
The drive is coming back and growing day by day
Winter is going to come to an end
I need to be prepared as all the lights turn on
I want to be remembered as one who always learned
Personally from mistakes, primarily from you!
Unconditionally my words do not provide justice
I can sing and I can write for you
The Staff.
          Let the Heart of David stand
And so my body stands alone
          Though I am one
          You who is in all things
          This is in me
You are my one and only
Now, I am one and lonely
          I came along
I wrote another song for you
          Only counting one, then two
          Because I am still in a daze
I don't belong
I am searching for this thing called truth
          I am asking, "Lord what should I do?"
          Find me a good place
I fear I will never figure out
How all this life is lived if not for love?
          I can best demonstrate
          How easy it can be to fill this heart so full of hate
And space, that is empty when the love is gone
It is misplaced. I read this back for you.
          True love irreplaceable.
          So we dance!

Red is the Color
Red is the best
So vivid her breast
So livid to test
The chest of my wife

Blue is the worst
Her fury alerts
The jury converts
The best for the knife

Yellow's my fellow
He stained the balloon
Who trained to be mellow
Yet remained full of strife

Green is so clean
Invisible to me
Invincible is my team
That fights for the light

Purple is the Kernel who
Tamed a Snap Turtle,
Who attempted to burrow
Into my motorbike

266. Into the People

People are reading more than ever
People talk, listen, read, and write
We are separated by a mighty class
More than age, more than race
More than sex, or even religion
War on the rich from the poor

Poor cling to the rich
They are afraid of the rich
What makes them so much better
My wealth is not of this world
My well if full
Full of unconditional love

Work, Church, School, Music

Take the time to breath
Continue to work hard
Pray for patience
Think of Her

Consider is pure joy

I am a tactile learner
I learn best through trial and error
Try to stay awake
Fight the sleeping monster
For she will come when you are weak and tired

If you tell the truth you don't have to remember anything

267. Ignorant Confidence

A man who loves fully
Prepares to dies at any time
The Lack of money the root of all evil
Living in a book most praise
Few know your strengths
Live by them
Believe in them
Become them
Tilt the scale weekly
Do not doubt
Have faith

An American speaking Christian

268. Rationality

        Physical, Mental, Social,
        Physics, Cognition, Policy
        Knowledge of Nature
        Process of acquiring knowledge
        Principles to achieve rational outcome

269. Irrationality

        Nothing, Atheism, Anarchy
        Hypothesis, and Theory
        Absence
        Infinite
        Immoral

270. Sleep

I wish I didn't have to sleep
I will sleep plenty when I am dead
I wander why God made us like this
Why give us bodies?
Why give us heads?

If I give you a book full of stories
But you can only read one story
And I have ten people read the same
Would you read on?

I leave behind childish ways
I remove the faults of youth
I lean towards zero tolerance
This is my preferred culture

I am excited about this new phase
I no longer need proof
Tell me your story
I am dancing towards the future

Describe to me what Testimony is
Give me yours
Attempt to be... to me...
Righteous, blameless, pure

Traci,
To love a human is strange
Love,
It comes in the strangest forms
It is a realm of endless wonder
Such a sweet soul
Proof,
A woman's love is more than enough

I have discovered
This relationship that holds great treasure
This country
We reward the brave
Be patient my brother
For God is love. Love is real

Story is natural for this human
Broken story, but story nonetheless
God links us through the power os story
God reveals himself through this power

Love,
The Love of God
Is Jesus God?
God is Love.
Jesus is Love...
Love is Real.
Jesus is Real
So he could be...
This does not bother me

What is the purpose of War if you do not love something?
None of us know what is going on.

The Story
I have been living in a daze
I have been living in a haze
I have been dreaming many dreams
I have considered many things
My DNA,
I am staring through the trees
Where the sun breaks the horizon
Many types of falling leaves
The Pine trees are Glowing Goldly
Most of the days
Today is different
The sky is grey
The leaves are changing
And falling and falling
It is cold
And winter is coming
The fire is also coming
Winter's Fire
The boy runs out to the woods
He is looking for his dog
He hears whimpering around the bend
And sees the snake slither away
He carries that old dog
Into his father's shop
He asks he could held
The boy's dad says, "fuck off"
And so we journey down
Onto the maker's road
To tell you friend a story
Of a time not long ago
I am good at telling stories
So everyone believes
There is magic in every word
Spoken for you and me

271. FergusonPoetryProject

The Beginning
The Dream of structure
The Structure upon the Foundation
The Philosophy behind the drive
The Heart of David begins to come alive

This is an exciting time
Full of love and laughter
Full of pain and tears
Yet, the future remains bright
In my May of Youth
The flowers begin to bloom

I see my mother growing old
She ages like wine
I see her raise group after group
Child after child
These children will impact the world

The continuing dreams
The continuing visions
The voice of the Lord
The coming of the Angels
We are beating our drums
We are singing in harmony

We are building a team
A band of brothers
We are teaching the young
Loving on another
We all have a past
This is understood
We will forgive on another
As we know we should

272. A Decade of Writing

I think I can say I will always write songs
I will always write excerpt of where I came from
I can honestly say that this life has been fair
It has given me opportunities impossible to compare

Life has been funny, but at some points very sad
Life has been luxurious and in some ways quite mad
I would not trade my life for any one thing
For love has me stumbling, head towards my feet

I have been writing poems for a decade now
I have written over a thousand poems
Some good and some bad
I have written on napkins, paper bags, and screens
I have written upon near most everything

My mind holds the music I try to translate
Within my head yearning for a great escape
I cannot begin to understand what it is for
I will write all day long, and in my dreams I write more

And so love takes my hand one time again
Love is so precious I cannot understand
How could one love someone troublesome like me
I do not complain because love is free

In a world shift towards capitalism
The rich will get richer
The poor will get poorer
The body will soon wither
The people of this country will go one of two ways
Being proud of the states
Or being filled with wretched hate

I will not be here to see it all unfold
I will hold on to love as I return to my home
I will patiently wait and watch from above
I will sing for you songs proclaiming, "you are enough!"

Time will no longer be measured
You will be consumed
You will no longer thirst
For I will always love you
I was taught this precious gift
From many people I loved
For they loved me also
And this was enough.

A decade has gone by
Cheers for another decade more
The curse has been broken
So now I may sore
Death will not cease me
I will forever live on
Through the people I loved
Through every inspired song

The Lord has been good
As he always has been
The Lord will be waiting
As will I to descend

For our family and friends
I will see you very soon
I love you so much
Sincerely, the Loon.

273. The Whiskey Family

How lucky are you?
I am, "The Loon"
The Mad Hatter's Apprentice
The son of the Moon

I have been here a while
Please come on in
Find yourself a seat
The show is about to begin

How lucky is me?
Under water I swim
In the fire I sing
In the air I defend
In the earth I feel free

I am drinking your whiskey
I am now feeling tipsy
Welcome to the tree
Whiskey Family

274. Just Another Day

Just another day
I return to the fields from long ago
I know I will be here a while
I am not sure what the future holds
All I can see is work

I must do what I love
So I can love what I do
Life is hard enough as it is
My life, my love, all need proof
All I can see if love

My head is spinning
My world is changing
I am approaching the end
The end of this beautiful road
All I can see is light

I hope they will remember
I hope they will understand
The simple poet's hope
For a future with his maid
All I can see is white

I can see work
I can see love
I can see light
I can see white

275. Back to the Basics (Translations of Translations)

I am still getting used to it
I am back where I was
She is here with me
It is everything I wanted
Yet, I am not whole
It is my heart
There is a hole in my heart
>It longs for my friend
>It longs for you
>I am here again
>Waiting for you
>But she is here
>And I love her still

I thank God for her
I thank God for everything
This is his world
These are his things
I give to the Boss what is his
But he will not have my heart
>Back to the basics my friend
>Learn how to write
>It does not need to rhyme
>I hardly rhyme in these writings
>This is on purpose
>It comes from what I have read
>Translations of the writings of David
>Translations of translations.

Learning and Learning

Come see
She is waiting for me
The songs still lay in my head

Be patient
Our turn will come
In time my friend

Wait here
Let us work hard
Work will bring us where we need to be

Life is hard
Life is weird
We learn and we learn
We take in what we choose

276. Friends of my Past

Never forget who came first if you're last
Never forget the friends of your past
Bring them together and have a good laugh
Reminisce about the world and hold fast

Five years flew by and so much has changed
Locations, occupations, and inspiration all changed
Hopefully I won't forget where I came from
Though through my life I have had many homes

I thank God every day for my soon to be wife
Her presence has brought to my eyes a new light
But I couldn't be the man I am today
Without the friends of my past

277. The Headache

The dull pain, the remains
The brain freeze, the frustration
The stress, the absurdities
The confusion, the dull pain

The headache that comes at the end of the day
The headache that comes when the day is far from over
The headache that comes when everybody is loud
The headache that comes when I need to be alone

I have never thought I would be here again
I love being a student, but I hate the system
I believe in my past life I was also a rebel
A rebel and a gypsy is all I have known

Maybe if I came inside?
Maybe if I just told her what I wanted?
Maybe we could come together as one?
Maybe, if I never knew the truth...
What if I never knew the truth?

278. <u>Haba Na Haba</u>

Continue to plan
        Though I know not tomorrow
Continue to dream
        Though the world turns to darkness
Continue to prosper
        Though the weight is pushing down
Continue to fight
        And Never Stop!

Little by little
        We walk through the fire
Little by little
        We will not be burned
Little by little
        We heal from the inside out
Little by little
        We find water in the drought

279. Sit Down and Write

I will begin to travel around the country
I am thinking long term
I do not care for one long venture
My life is an adventure
My life will continue
Even after I am gone
I had the opportunity
And so I seized it

Let's bring in all my friends
Bring them in one at a time
Enter into this world
Where all can feel alive
Cut me loose!

Slowly they are coming
Slowly they are arriving
What is this story going to be about?
Let us find out

I am because you are
She and I have so much fun
Because we were, I am now
I am now because I was with you

She will realize she is far too good for me
I realized it too
She will see she is far too clean for me
I will agree with you

Share with the design
And wait for her return
Show her mercy all of the time
And never let her burn

280. The FireTower and Cherokee

And so we yelled down from the firetower
We saw the billows of smoke in the sky
Coffee in abundance
The white tails flying high

I have had my share of chocolate
The chicken is on the grill
The wine was fulfilling
The morning had its chill

Today was a good day
A strange on upon the lake
A place I will see again
On a later date

Time to make the dinner
And to settle down again
With a wonderful woman
And a guitar in my hand

Footage

I ask her about her day and she says,
"Why?"
She wants to know what I am doing
My incentive is not as clear as the goal in mind
She is cleaning all of the dishes
Alabama was at our fingertips today
We danced around Lake Martin
The wood all torn down
By the tornados long forgotten

And so they built these condos
We cook and drink our wine
We think about the future
She reads this while standing behind me

281. Memory #7-

It's coming
It stands in the closet
It stares at me through the bathroom
It watches in silence
     It appears in my rooms
     Floating inches above the floor
     I could call it a ghost
     But then some of you wouldn't believe
I recall my dream
It appears again
I recall each scene
Step by step I should win
     Stage after stage I play and I die
     To start at the beginning just one more time
     I get to the rope and I try to swing
I fall to the bottom; impaled by sharp things

282. Comfortable and Concerned

How do we push forward this time?
Age catches up with me as I grow tired
Baby Blue says it's all over now
I couldn't remember what she needed
     I ran through today
     I am exhausted as the sun dips down
     I am remembering the lyrics to this old song
     They surface from time to time
I am overstimulated
I am covered in love
I am worn out from the day
I have not been caring for myself
     They say to not completely empty the cup
     They say to save some
     I can't remember the rest
     I can hardly remember anything anymore
These years caught up like a flood
I am now in the middle of what I thought was fairy tale
The time is coming where all lend all
My last memory of Sir Waters
     I painted it once more
     I smeared wet ash on the face of my enemy
     The voices were gone
     One remained, speaking of a man

283. An Excerpt from the Book of Man

He was the first in his eyes
She was the second in hers
One can only serve for so long
They knew the best of the best
And the worst of the worst

I can't recall the first time
I remember ours
I do not care about yours
I only care for you
And us

My soul is lost inside this room
My memories begin to fade
Was it all real?
Was it all just a dream really?

I do not miss it
I am fond of the memories
I do not miss the man I was
I'm still excited for the man to come
I love the woman she has become

Time is moving forward faster and faster
Overestimate what you can do in a year
Underestimate what you can do in ten
But my patience is wearing thin
My patience has come to an end

284. Surveys Upon Surveys

The path is emerging from the stories all told
Two stories emerging to form "the Alchemist's" Gold
"The World As I Know It" begins to unfold
And Philo himself would refer it as bold

I am stirring up memories from so long ago
I remember old faces and friends I let go
I am stepping away from awkward repetition
I am stepping up to the plate with a song I call "Vincent"

People would refer to him as a young Nat King Cole
He may be a white boy, but he sure got soul
My teachers all work hard and they're just like me
Some raised in the South, and some raised as Yankees

I keep singing these rough songs like Mr. Robert
I keep dreaming these dreams of diamond sealed Pearls
For now, I'll just sit here eating my cheap fast food
To give me a few more moments before I talk to you

Survey these people to see what they like
What works for the group is essentially right?

285. As One

Sometimes we listen when we are not
It's so hard to find things in the dark
There can be evil in what we say
But let's not worry about what comes our way

We all know how this ends
Let's take the road to happiness
You and I both run
Let's come together as One

Man-made land scape for us to keep
Let's celebrate!
Let's celebrate!
All we have done is come together as one
Let's celebrate!
Let's celebrate!

Sometimes we see them, illusions
Of what is right and what is wrong
It fools us
I guarantee this life has more meaning
This hate surrounds us, overflowing

We all know how this ends
Let's take the road to happiness
You and I both run
Let's come together as One

Man-made land scape for us to keep
Let's celebrate!
Let's celebrate!
All we have done is come together as one
Let's celebrate!
Let's celebrate!

The Transition

My Friend
Carry on
Take these words and write more songs
Live more life and carry on

My love
Take my hand
Forever we will laugh and dance
Forever we will have to wait

My brother
Walk the line
Think of me and start to cry
Only tears of joy

286. Troublesome Mind

Baby, I can hardly resist the way your soft lips kiss
Take me on a journey somewhere far
Maybe train, plane, or car
I was thinking we could go someplace
A place that you don't know...

Sit and watch the stars,
No need for a phone
Because your eyes shine so bright
Under this beautiful night sky...

And I know that you are mine

Girl, just sit down next to me
Our next stop will be heavenly
Can't believe I can call you mine
And OH, how you soothe my troublesome mind

287. Sword High

Making my way back to where we first met
Memories of you are running through my head
Like some lonesome child I say my prayers
Wishing my hands were running through your hair

It may be too far to drive your car
But baby look at the moon, I am not very far
Keep your sword high

Baby I know it is hard to believe
That night we danced on the beach
Your eyes they shine so bright
As my love for you soared so high

288. Come Before

Come before
    all your friends
        serve them well
Lend your hand
    You know us guys
        We must go
Protect the girls
    Who love us so
        Pick up your hat
Say a prayer
    We struggle hard
        On this lovely pair
Of life and death
    It surrounds us all
        In this world
We grow and fall

But OH, how I long to see my destiny
We call forth within his eyes
That beautiful moment when we must fly

289. Star Crossed Intimacy

Seal it with your cursed love
Because these hands don't grab with gloves
And girl come back to me
Because this loving makes us feel so free
> You are higher than the morning sun
> Shining, saying, "Let's have some fun!"

So careful, what you say
Because your momma doesn't mind
What comes our way
Let's escape
Find a peaceful place
We can burn till we can't feel our face

290. I'd Like to Say

Sitting here, by myself one day
Saw a girl across the way
I'd like to take you out sometime
If that is all right

We can go anywhere you want to
We can tell jokes all night
I've been alone recently
Could use a little company

I would like to say it's beautiful today
We can do anything you want to
Staying in my mind, won't even reply
Chilling here waiting for you
Chilling here waiting for you

Her eyes are lighting up with the sunrise
I could watch it everyday
I promise girl, I am interested
In learning more about your way
And maybe you could take the time
The time to get to know me

I think she is shy
She doesn't know how
I just want to make her smile
I just want to make her smile

Because girl
Let's see everything
Meant to be in this world
And believe me when I say
Everything about you
Makes me weak to my knees
Baby please, understand
We can be something that's unplanned

The Summit
Few will make it to see the view
Few will make it out
This love is for the few

291. Saying Something About a Bridge

He says, "Why that?"
"Why this for the bridge?"

292. I Bet You Would Say

I dream of her practicing the saxophone
She is trying to not wake anyone in the house
I bet you would say it is hard to remember
I bet you would say I didn't talk much

I bet you would say, "Me and him? We ain't nothing! Baby!"

That autumn breeze remains
I can still remember
 I may have still been sane
It was raining last November
I cannot complain though
It brought up many questions
It brought up everything about you

-I bet you'd say it's hard to remember
(Oh, I don't remember you)
I bet you'd say we didn't talk much
(Me and him, we ain't nothing baby)

293. The Perfect Place

On the water, eyes blind
Yet, free as your mind
Shouldn't we unwind?
        Listen to the subtle jazz
        Playing in the background
        The sun goes down in this packed cab
Hovering above the water
Lift off, and take sail
The waves they soothe us, they never fail

        A picture is wanted
        Family needs it for pleasure
        Stuck in this moment we cannot measure
                Oh, this wonderful place
                There is nothing better

The fragrance of the breeze
Ease a red tent
Clouds and the sky
Graze like a sweet peppermint
        Reflection on the water like a mirror a rose
        Like a pedal upon a troubled stone

Live it like you are dying
Don't you wait
This perfect place
You cannot repaint

294. The Wind

        Come to me wind
        Let me smell your sweet scented breeze
        Bring me the warmth of your spring, wind
        Flowers bloom, pollenated by the bees
        As spring rolls around, make a beautiful blend

        Show me the way you blow the grass
        Remember how you make the sky so blue?
        Loosen the beautiful life and the enclosed night
        Loosen the light thin clouds and the burning sky
        Beg mother nature to let your beauty fly high

295. Mother

I was just a young boy
Jumping on the trampoline,
Waiting on my momma to come
Tell me it's cold and dinner is ready

She said, "Son,
Why are you going out there with no jacket?
Boy, don't ya know you're gonna get sick?"
                I didn't care for the moment
                I didn't care for the moment

                She loves you to the break of dawn
                And memories fade until they are gone
                Be good to one another
                And always love your mother

So many things in life we take for granted
Dwell on being less than perfect
But we must try everyday
You know there is one person who will take care of you
When you are bed ridden, sick with the flu,
                Nobody is perfect, but she is closer than you
                Nobody is perfect, but she is closer than you

                She loves you to the break of dawn
                And memories fade until they are gone
                Be good to one another
                And always love your mother

I Can Hear the Song
It is beginning to play
The song for the end of days
As my time runs out
The song gets louder

I can hear it louder and louder every day
The song that is my life
The song that is our life
Because this is our band

This love is so real
I want you to listen hard and feel it
This love is for all
But not all will receive it

296. The Lovely Dream

I saw it
        Thirty years
It was strange and surreal
        Thirty years of life well lived
I saw it
        Both of them
It was perfect. It was everything
        Seven years of hard work
The lovely dream came during the day
My phone rang not long after
Her voice spoke, "You can know me"
I know you
        She spoke again,
"Do not be afraid. Love me."
I love you
        She turned again
Time flew by as a blink of an eye

I smiled
        She smiled
We were both awake
        I laughed
She laughed
        I made bacon bit pancakes
They woke and came down
        I was forty

297. Comprehension

There are not enough words my love
All of this time and I still do not know you
You told me, you promised, you convinced me
Daily you surprise me

How long until I can know you completely?
Just like falling in love
It seems like I am daily falling in love
It seems that I am failing to show you

Three long years
And now I am on year 2 of 7
Until that dream come true
Until that star shines through

She begs you for a relationship
Something more than just physical
Something more than just emotional
Something more than just social

For the first time he understands
For the first time he comprehends
For the first time
For the last time

298. Oil and Water

Oil and water do not mix
The oils on my fingertips rust these strings
Crossroads, Brickhouse, Grazing Here
Burgers, French Fries, Ice Cold Beer
I find myself in a familiar place
It seems to be crossing through time and space
I will go back to a lonely room
Waiting for the weekend
I am waiting look into your eyes
I cannot wait to see the shapes and colors
All I need resides in those eyes

My hands are bloodied from today's work
My fingertips are bloodied from last night's work
My face is scratched from the limbs of mighty trees
My heart is torn from demons and things

I am off to the mountains again
I am following my heart North
I am running far from this city
I am cursing the tide that pulls her away

Walk on water and slip on oil
Cover yourself and head down under
We are clean and dirty loving one another
We are peeling off surfaces and removing covers

299. Just Getting Started

How did it all begin?
It is hard to remember…
      Some big events, a lot of little events
      They all lead up to this moment
Time and time again

Where did we meet?
I can barely remember…
      Was it this stage or that stage?
      Was it here or there?
Stage and stage again

We are just getting started my friend
Time and time again we push forward
We beat the odds taking over stage after stage
We are just getting started

300. The Curse is Broken

Thank you my friend for the time has come
I'll see you the next time I come home
The curse is broken and I am free
Off into the world to see new things

To learn new things, to chase new dreams
To truly become all I can be
To fight for life and love and peace
To fight for God and You and Me

The curse is broken my dearest friend
The Eye welcomes You home again
You and I praising the earth and the sky
The love of our Lord pouring out as light

The curse is broken, so I move on
I will return when the moon covers the sun
The Owl will hoot and the sky will be clear
My spirit will be in you and your vision become clear

Love is real, it is here, it is now
Love is all I need right now
My comfort is in the lovers out there
Split like Horcruxes within thin air

But there is one who makes me whole
It makes me completely lose control
The Heart of David is for now complete
Until eternity, where our hearts will meet
                Once Again

And so, here we are again. Standing on the remains of what used to be a battleground. We stand here victorious. For today, we have won the battle, but we will not forget that this minute of peace is preparing us for the upcoming war. We are building upon this foundation little by little; day by day. All of these songs are stories. All of the stories are songs. All of these stories were told by the people who lived them with the people who witnessed them. These are all of the people in my life who desired nothing but love. Love is what connects us all. Love is the common ground. Love is what build Southern Ground. The desire to love and to be love. The desire to become something new, and the desire to believe in something more.

I have had the pleasure of having many wonderful teachers up to this point. They have shaped and molded my mind to be part of a greater body. Friends and Family, Brothers and Sister, Enemies and Lovers… let us celebrate and enjoy the world!

No race, age, or sex will take away from the love we share. People who truly know love and the language of Music will always find a place to call home. This world will be given to darkness forever one day, but those who learn who to communicate with the angels will be spared from the darkness by becoming light. And… Light will always find Light.

A list of names remains with me at all times. I am truly grateful for every name on the list. These are the people who made me who I am today. Some of these names no longer walk the earth. (may those friends live through me). And when I am gone, I will live through you and so on. This is the foundation of our faith, my brothers. This is the foundation of our faith, my sisters. This Love is the cornerstone of our faith. From Abraham and Isaac and Jacob, through Moses and Joshua and down the latter, to all of the patriarchs were able to do so, to all of the writers and poets who stumbled into grace, may peace be with you. I am because you are. We are because they were.

The last thing to say is that Mankind has found a way to achieve immortality through discipleship. This is true. This is outstanding. If ever there was a better time to live than in the New World, then I am unaware. Things could be better, but things could be much, much worse. This United State of Freedom will forever breed world class workers, musicians, artists, and lovers of the light.

We the people are one.

END

Follow the Course

Throughout this journey titled, "The Heart of David" one is taken through a life of a common teenager steamrolling into adulthood. There are twists and turns, philosophies and friendships, thoughts on love and hate, thoughts on life and death, politics and religion, lovers and enemies, and common blends of the rational and the irrational. This book is documented as being written over the course of twelve years plus years, with the direct help of over a dozen or so people, and a direct influence of over one hundred and forty-four people.

Following the Course is a way to better understand what the purpose of the FergusonPoetryProject is. There is a mission of respecting the songwriters of the past, but the main mission is bringing people together. Whether it is through food, music, or fellowship, the FergusonPoetryProject is going to be able to find the common ground through love. The Heart of David is a way of finding spirituality in the simplest form through healthy worship while balancing physical, social, and mental/emotional health. Healthiness is happiness, and "happiness is only real when shared". –Christopher McCandless.

This is the living Journal of J. Arthur Ferguson...

...a few Credits...

Benjamin David Boyd	Bryan Lee Mays	Kolton Ray Stooksbury
	Patrick	
Eric	Blake	Jacob
Sam	Mclane	Luke
Tyler	Bobby	Kyler
Sean	Jeff	Tristan
Connor	Michael	Kent
Jackson	Austin	Thom
Johnny	Brandon	Nick
Jon	Terry	Donald
George	Dylan	Peter
Hal	Tony	Justin
Jack	John	Brody
James		Mike

RIP

Jeff	Josh	Chase